Interventions and Provocations

D1343084

3 8025 00608471 2

SUNY Series,
INTERRUPTIONS: Border Testimony(ies)
and Critical Discourse/s

Henry A. Giroux, Editor

Interventions and Provocations

Conversations on Art, Culture, and Resistance

Edited by
Glenn Harper

YORK ST. JOHN
LIBRARY & INFORMATION
SERVICES

WITHDRAWN

0 1 MAY 2023

STATE UNIVERSITY OF NEW YORK PRESS

Cover: Photograph of Guillermo Gómez-Peña in *Temple of Confessions*, a work by Guillermo Gómez-Peña and Roberto Sifuentes. Courtesy of Detroit Institute of Art.

Interviews reprinted by permission of *Atlanta Art Papers, Inc.*

Production by Ruth Fisher
Marketing by Fran Keneston

Published by
State University of New York Press, Albany

© 1998 State University of New York

All rights reserved

Printed in the United States of America

No part of this book may be used or reproduced in any manner whatsoever without written permission. No part of this book may be stored in a retrieval system or transmitted in any form or by any means including electronic, electrostatic, magnetic tape, mechanical, photocopying, recording, or otherwise without the prior permission in writing of the publisher.

For information, address the State University of New York Press, State University Plaza, Albany, NY 12246

Library of Congress Cataloging-in-Publication Data

Interventions and provocations : conversations on art, culture, and
    resistance / edited by Glenn Harper.
        p.   cm. — (SUNY series, interruptions — border
    testimony(ies) and critical discourse/s)
        Includes index.
        ISBN 0-7914-3725-6 (hc : acid-free paper). — ISBN 0-7914-
    3726-4 (pb : acid-free paper)
        1. Artists—United States–Interviewed. 2. Arts, American.
    3. Arts, Modern—20th century—United States. I. Harper, Glenn,
    1946-   .   II. Series.
    NX504.I58   1998
    700'.973'0904—dc21   97-32761
                                                              CIP

10   9   8   7   6   5   4   3   2   1

Contents

Introduction

Although the discourse on contemporary art has been dominated in the 1980s and '90s by Postmodern pastiche and a sometimes facile critique of consumerism, throughout the past two decades there have been a number of artists who have been engaged in creating a form of art that exhibits a Postmodern skepticism about transcendence but nevertheless seeks to engage critically and creatively with society and history. These artists have sought to forge new relations among art, everyday life, and the public sphere. Their work is not related in terms of style, gallery affiliations, regional groupings, or promotional groupings created by the art press. They are instead related to one another by the critical approach they take toward social norms, and by their resistance to centralized cultural hegemony. This alternative to the art market and to the culture of passive consumption is characterized by the artists' interventions in and challenges to everyday social reality.

The interventionist and provocationist artists participate in a new invigoration of public space and civic discourse (sometimes with results far beyond the usually narrow borders of the art world, such as in the public debates over the works of Andres Serrano, Karen Finley, and Tim Miller, all of whose voices can be heard in the conversations collected in this volume). Whether these artists' site of engagement is the gallery or the street, they participate in the creation of a new form of art that is conceptual rather than object-oriented; unlike classic conceptual art, however their work attempts to influence a public beyond the galleries and art magazines— but at the same time, unlike overtly political art, their work avoids both ideology and any belief in utopian, transcendental goals. Whether their work is performance, installation, text, painting, sculpture, film, or the kind of public collaboration that Arlene Raven has called "art in the public interest," these artists are involved in the creation of a new form of art that is both public and skeptical.

That is to say, the political interventions and social provocations exemplified by the artists in this collection demonstrate an attitude toward art and form that can be characterized as "tactical," adopting a term used by Michel de Certeau, or "postutopian," a term used by Boris Groys to describe the unofficial art of the late Soviet Union. These artists have lost the early twentieth century's faith in radical transformations and transcendental ideals. They have not abandoned the ambition of twentieth-century artists to engage with the social realm, but they are much more likely to see the social impact of their work as an intervention into the network of normal social relations or a provocation to normative social values.

The relation to daily life staked out by these artists owes a great deal to Bertolt Brecht and Viktor Shklovsky for the idea that art produces an alienation or estrangement that interrupts the flow of normal, normative, socialized experience. But it is perhaps not coincidental that these artists began to appear during a revival of interest in Mikhail Bakhtin, the Soviet critic whose notions of answerability, dialogism, and the carnivalesque suggest that art must be engaged with daily life, but also that art's transfiguration of an audience's experience will be a momentary, liminal experience rather than a revolutionary transformation.

The practice of tactical artists can be categorized as feminist, political, performative, or even "puerile," to borrow a term from Peter Schjeldahl's *Village Voice* columns. But unlike artists intent on realizing an essential feminine, a political truth, or a return of the repressed desires of childhood, postutopian artists use tactics like provocation in the service of critical interventions in social discourse. For example, Nayland Blake's soft sculpture installations engage in a breadth of dialogue with daily life that is beyond Mike Kelley's intentions in the stuffed animal installations and other "puerile" works for which the latter artist is famous. Blake brings both his own life and his political engagement into his work in ways that Kelley does not, in spite of the power of Kelley's aesthetic explorations of repression, representation, and the art world itself. Blake's work derives its power from the autobiographical exploration, political commitment, and depth of both vision and humor that the artist exhibits throughout all phases of his work.

The formal aspects of this work also represent a shift within the avant-garde. The concept of artistic form in both the making of a postutopian art and the discussions surrounding such art suggests the use of the word "form" by the Polish novelist Witold Gombrowicz in his novels and diaries from the 1930s to the '60s. Gombrowicz uses form in a double sense, to refer to aesthetic form and to social form, by which he means the social masks that we create to give others the impression of a unified subject and which we ultimately come to believe in ourselves. That is to say, form is both aestheticization and socialization, and the social agent and the artist both are form makers and prisoners of form. Gombrowicz is both seduced and repelled by form, which he associates with maturity, and the only alternative he sees to form or maturity is the equally ambiguous category of youth or immaturity. Youth in his sense is the embodiment of precisely the violent, messy, temporary, energetic, diverse, and chaotic qualities that artists like Kathy Acker rely upon in their search for an art that is "more than craft, more than decorations for the people in power." (Acker, "Models of Our Present," *Artforum* 22:6, May 1984, pp. 62–65)

The postutopian interventionist and provocationist artists have embraced this "youthful" impropriety in their attack on social and aesthetic form, while at the same time maintaining a Gombrowiczean skepticism about both the rigid "form" of social and aesthetic norms and any alternative disruption of them. They have adopted a tactical approach to social and aesthetic interventions. This approach may be seen to be grounded in the work of de Certeau, who made a distinction between strategy and tactics in the practice of everyday life (and de Certeau also singles out Gombrowicz as the creator of the hero of the fleeting politics and pleasures of tactics). de Certeau says that "a strategy assumes a place that can be circumscribed as proper.... Political, economic, and scientific rationality has been constructed on this model.... [A] 'tactic,' on the other hand,...cannot count on a 'proper.'.... A tactic insinuates itself into the other's place, fragmentarily, without taking it over in its entirety, without being able to keep it at a distance.... [A] tactic...is always on the watch for opportunities that must be seized 'on the wing.' Whatever it wins, it does not keep. It must constantly manipulate events in order to turn them into opportunities" (*The Practice of Everyday Life*, tr. Steven Rendall. Berkeley: University of California Press, 1984, p. xix). For de Certeau, tactics are the means by which the consumers at the receiving end of social production manipulate everyday life for their own purposes. The artists of tactics are in solidarity with these tactical consumers, with respect to their relation to central power structures, and also with their relation to daily life.

The art of tactics seeks a new relation to everyday life; sometimes that relation takes the form of collaboration with communities beyond the art world, sometimes the form of political intervention of a distinctly postutopian character. Sometimes these tactics involve provocations that are not overtly political but have political consequences, and sometimes they simply adopt new forms of public address.

For tactical artists, daily life is a contested territory, not a taken-for-granted horizon for their life or work. But they do not project a global, ideological, alternative life-world through their work. In a similar way, according to Boris Groys, the "sots art" of Komar and Melamid and other manifestations of late Soviet-era Russian art achieve their unique character by rejecting the utopian claims of both the classical Russian avant-garde and Stalinist social realism (*The Total Art of Stalinism: Avant-Garde, Aesthetic Dictatorship, and Beyond*, tr. Charles Rougle. Princeton: Princeton University Press, 1992). But Groys does not see the work of Komar and Melamid, Ilya Kabakov, or Erik Bulatov as apolitical or solipsistic (as some poststructuralist or postmodern positions might be characterized, due to a paralyzing skepticism about authenticity, the genuine, or political action). Their own skepticism about authenticity and action and subjectivity impels them toward a comic or frivolous (though nonetheless serious) engagement with contemporary life. Kabakov in particular exhibits a profound engagement with *homo sovieticus*, and the situation in which his characters find themselves has not disappeared with the decline of the Soviet state. His work, as Groys suggests, emphasizes individual voices rather than collective ideologies of the right or the left. The same might be said of other artists whose work derives from Western rather than Soviet sources. Fred Wilson, for instance, is known for his installations critiquing museums and museology, but his work also gives voice to the stories of individuals silenced by racism and colonialism. Wilson does not speak for them, he finds ways to bring these individuals forward to speak for themselves. The interview with Wilson in this collection provides examples of both his work and his manner of working.

Some other contemporary artists in the West are taking up a similar position by locating art in communication and social interaction rather than the enclosed space of the self, which has historically been projected into social space by artists only in the enclave of the gallery. The artists in this collection of interviews have all sought, through interventions into political space or provocations directed at social space, to create a disorder, impropriety, or interaction directed toward social change that is real, though not revolutionary. All of the artists in this collection have exhibited an effective resistance to the numbing force of mass society, and all of them have also proposed active alternatives, countervisions of human life at the end of the industrial age. There are, of course, tactical differences among them: most of the artists interviewed in the first half of the collection have chosen to address social concerns through direct confrontations with issues, practices, and contradictions raised by the society at large; the artists in the second half may not create work that is explicitly political in content, but it nevertheless constitutes a challenge to society's norms through strategies that are provocative in the use of sexuality, religion, race, or gender.

Art's social role has been actively contested in the United States in the 1980s and '90s, in large part through the interventions into public discourse carried out by tactical and postutopian artists. Ironically, the assumption underlying the resulting attacks on political art and government arts funding, mostly from the right wing of the political spectrum, is that art has an active influence on the fabric of society—thus, the importance of art has been emphasized rather than diminished in the public controversies surrounding the National Endowment for the Arts and a number of provocationist artists (often those using homosexual themes or explicit sexuality). This backhanded endorsement of the power of art has occurred within a climate in which political forces of the right *and* the left have frequently hoped for an art that would be a passive reflection of social goals rather than an active force in its own right, and in which the broad audience for art has often gravitated toward work that is decorative and optimistic rather than political and aggressive. The artists in this volume, on the other hand, assert the vitality of art as a political act, yet they achieve in their work an art that cannot be described as simple didacticism. They appropriate the power of art and they project the depth of their political convictions at the same time. Guillermo Gómez-Peña states (in the conversation included in this volume) that "in the '90s we as artists can conquer more central spaces to speak from, and function as cross-cultural diplomats, as counter-journalists, as border pirates, as experimental activists." All of the artists and theorists interviewed in this volume operate in the simultaneously central and marginal zone described by Gómez-Peña; all of them have contested mainstream culture at its very base, in the imagination and vision that makes culture itself possible.

All of these interviews appeared originally in *Art Papers*, a magazine founded in 1977 as the newsletter of the Atlanta Art Workers Coalition. *Art Papers* has over the past twenty years increasingly emphasized contemporary art as a field of action and inquiry, rather than as an idealized site of aesthetic activity. Although the magazine has from its inception covered the work of artists from the entire spectrum of contemporary art (from the political to the formal to the philosophical), the activism inherent in the name of its original parent organization has remained a vital element of the magazine.

Through five shifts in the position of editor-in-chief, through shifts in the orientation of art in three succeeding decades, the writers and artists involved in the production of *Art Papers* have remained dedicated to a basic opposition to anti-intellectual, socially regressive, and politically repressive forces in the art world and in society at large. As a result, *Art Papers* has remained at the forefront of both contemporary art and the presentation of postutopian artists such as those included in this volume.

The regional character of *Art Papers* has also been a factor in its commitment to tactical artists. Based in Atlanta, *Art Papers* is not only "outside New York" but planted in the middle of a "New South" that is characterized more by commercial ambition than cultural achievement. The audience for contemporary art is widely scattered in the southern United States, and the need and desire for communication with other artists and with a diverse, widely distributed audience has fostered an understanding of both a grassroots journal like *Art Papers* and new ways of making and discussing art.

The interviews collected here are only a snapshot of the magazine's publishing history. Articles by some of the most interesting writers on art today (some well known, others too little known), the most extensive and diverse review section of any U.S. art magazine, lively consideration of the daily working lives of artists, and the presentation of new artwork (in the form of "artists' pages" designed specifically for presentation in *Art Papers*) continue as important aspects of the publication. *Art Papers* is also oversized, demonstrating its origin as a tabloid newspaper and also the origins of art criticism in the popular press. In format as well as content, *Art Papers* is focused on process rather than product, work on culture rather than works in museums.

Like those of us who have kept *Art Papers* going for more than twenty years, the artists in this collection recognize some hard truths. There has to be communication with a public that we know is largely not interested in difficult ideas, but we know easy ideas can't convey difficult truths; we know image-saturated culture overwhelms the critical thought that is necessary to keep our culture and ourselves alive; and we know that outrageous art will reinforce the arguments of the "culture cleansers" of the political right, but also that only outrageous art can bring critical thought to the attention of a public not interested in difficult ideas. We have to be tentative and unrelenting; we have to do serious work on culture by interacting with everyday life, in ways that won't earn us a living. These artists' work, whether confrontational or community-based in its particular expression, embodies a solidarity with social groups that are the target of authoritarian strategies, as well as embodying action oriented toward bringing social relations to consciousness. The forms in which their tactics are expressed are constantly absorbed into the mainstream arts, media, and culture, the total system of the information age. But the tactics themselves survive, seeking to express not an "outside" so much as an "everywhere-always-particular" position: a position that keeps alive critical thought and skeptical perspective with relation to globalizing social forms; that tactical position is their significant contribution to the cultural life of the next millennium.

Acknowledgments

I owe a great debt of gratitude to the interviewers and interviewees whose participation over the past ten years has made this volume (and the issues of *Art Papers* in which these conversations were originally published) possible. I also want to thank the current and former staff of *Art Papers* for their dedicated efforts to create and sustain the journal, including (roughly in the order of their participation in the magazine): Julia Fenton, Dan Talley, Laura Lieberman, Xenia Zed, Ellen Stewart, Barbara Schreiber, Amy Jinkner-Lloyd, Linda Adams-Plante, Allison Ritch, Alan Sondheim, Meg Governo, Jerry Cullum, Virginia Warren Smith, Elizabeth Lide, Betty Emrey, Mildred Thompson, Carolyn Griffin, Marymay Impastato, Ashley Wisner, Anne Leeds, Cathy Downey (the current managing editor), Pattie Belle Hastings, Bjørn Akselsen, Michele Slater, Ruth Resnicow (the current editor-in-chief), Michael Pittari, Jennifer Smith, and Elizabeth

Sawyer (whose proofreading of this book saved us from numerous errors). Many others have provided essential help in publishing the journal over the years, including the dedicated *Art Papers* Board of Directors, hundreds of writers and artists, and numerous volunteers, friends, and advisors. And, finally, thanks to Henry Giroux, editor of the "Interruptions: Border Testimony(ies) and Critical Discourse/s" series, and Priscilla Ross, of the State University of New York Press, for making the publication of this book possible.

Glenn Harper, former editor of *ART PAPERS*, currently editor
of *SCULPTURE* magazine

1

Guillermo Gómez-Peña

Interviewed by Mildred Thompson

Guillermo Gómez-Peña is a performance artist known for his cross-cultural texts, including performances as a borderland disk jockey of the future and as a cultural artifact (such as in Year of the White Bear, *in which he and artist Coco Fusco exhibited themselves as recently discovered aboriginal Amerindians in the lobby of several museums, including the Smithsonian's Museum of Natural History). He was born in Mexico City and relocated to California in 1978. Since that time, his installations and performances have consistently interrogated the cultures of the Americas with incisive wit and provocative political analysis. A major source of the powerful effect he achieves in his work is his refusal to allow the audience a formal vantage point from which they view "objectively" the social situation in which they are in fact always intimately implicated. His point of view draws in a whole panoply of racial backgrounds, popular culture, social action, formal creativity, and a theatrical embodiment of individual human life. His work is the inherently provocative incarnation of the edgy, energetic postutopian America of the next millennium. He has received a MacArthur Foundation Grant, among other awards. Gómez-Peña has also published a book of his writings,* Gringostroika Warrior, *and a two-CD set of his radio works,* Borderless Radio. *The following conversation took place in 1993.*

Mildred Thompson: The set for some of your performances, a dead chicken hanging, feathers, and candles, is itself very strong. Do these elements have a definite symbolism?

Guillermo Gómez-Peña: In terms of the chicken, there is of course a literal meaning that I am particularly interested in, but that doesn't exclude other possibilities. The literal meaning is that in Spanish the migrant workers are derogatorily referred to as *pollos*—chickens. In the thirties, the Texas Rangers used to hang migrant workers. So the image of the hanging chicken is a very powerful and sinister archetypal image of violence towards migrant workers. So that is perhaps the first reading of the image. But since a lot of the work I do explores the territory of cultural misunderstanding, and the border is also one in which symbols crack open and metaphors dilute or fracture or reshape themselves, I also welcome misreadings of the chicken. One common misreading is that of the use of the chicken in witchcraft, *santeria*, voodoo, *candomblé*, which often scares people. Many times in past performances where I have used dead chickens on the stage, people have this stereotypical image of the chicken as an object for witchcraft. And in the history of the South, as Keith Antar Mason has reminded me, African Americans would be hanged for stealing chickens.

Thompson: And the candles and feathers?

Gómez-Peña: As far as the feathers go, most of the characters I work with at Highways Performance Space are mixtures of multiple traditions, but all together they create a kind of cyber-identity, a kind of pastiche of identities, and I hope to embody these multiple identities on a stage. This particular character I'm working with, El Aztec High-Tech, has a very stylized mariachi suit which I designed, an Aztec headdress, a number of buttons coming from all political causes, heavy metal paraphernalia, the chest piece, and these very stylized dark glasses, this low rider touch, this Chicano touch. So I am very interested in creating characters which are hybrids. Each character contains a multiplicity of selves and carries a multiplicity of traditions on the stage. In terms of the candles—

I think that I am very much interested in a kind of portable theater, in a theater that can fit in a suitcase, low-tech theater—creating a total experience out of very simple elements. Candles have always been powerful sources for transforming the environment in a very rich way, in a way that electric lights cannot possibly do. And they are also sources of concentration for us. Every time that we lose concentration on the stage, we just look at the candles.

Thompson: The use of the boombox tape recorder was very reminiscent of *Krapp's Last Tape*—one man on a stage with a tape recorder, and him talking into it. But Beckett's stage setting doesn't have the symbolism, just the guy with the tape recorder.

Gómez-Peña: Working it out. Trying to deal with who he is and how he's become what he's become. Until you said it, I hadn't seen the relationship.

Thompson: Krapp records everything he's going through, and he plays back and plays forward, and it's his own voice— do you use that often?

Gómez-Peña: Yes. In the mid-'80s many performance colleagues felt that performance art had become so artificial, so infra-structurally and technically complex that we really needed to go back to the basics once more, to recapture the spoken word, to do work that was easily tourable, and also to go back to the basic items of popular culture. People in Mexico, just like in the African-American community, utilize the ghetto blaster in many ways; the ghetto blaster has multiple functions. A ghetto blaster in a car can turn the car into a nightclub. A ghetto blaster in a park can turn the park into a party. Walking down the street with a ghetto blaster, you can make an existential statement. The ghetto blaster becomes a companion, an extension of yourself, an extension of your mind; through the radio you view other realities. And the idea that the ghetto blaster is a musical instrument is something I've been working with since the mid-'80s. I arrive on stage with a couple of tapes, and I can switch from English radio to Spanish radio to one tape, change tapes, then go back to radio, and then intertwine my text into the radio and the musical patterns coming out of the ghetto blaster. I use it very much as a musical instrument. Also, because I really get inspired by popular culture, youth with ghetto blasters completely inspires me.

Thompson: I find that your whole theme is prophetic. Do you feel that what you are saying is a prophecy, your relationship to the migration of the Mexicans?

Gómez-Peña: Before 1988, my world view was very utopian. Since the big smoke began, the big change, of the last four years, a change that I began just artificially to locate as beginning in the Tiananmen Square massacre—and that led to several international incidents, the fall of the Berlin Wall, the fall of "real socialism," the fall of several Latin American dictatorships, the invasion of Panama, the cease-fire in El Salvador, the L.A. insurrection—we have been dealing with four years of incredible complexity when we have been unable to digest anything. And I find that what has happened in my work is that my vision has become distorted. Basically, the kind of world I am trying to articulate in recent texts is what I call end-of-the-century society. Of course I push reality to extremes, and I tend to interweave it with fiction. As I put it in one of the lines of the performance, we are living in a cyberpunk film directed by José Martí and Ted Turner. Yes, I do believe that we are living unprecedented changes at an incredible speed, and we are perplexed by them. Every day I wake up and I turn on the TV, and a major structural change in the world has taken place, and I haven't even digested the one of the night before.

Thompson: It appears that these are isolated incidents, the fall of the Berlin Wall and so on. Do you feel that it's really all the same force?

Gómez-Peña: In a sense, I feel that these are really the birth pangs of the new millennium. And especially now—we have been talking about the need to create the epic of the end of the century, the need to find an epic voice to describe this epic drama—we are living now through a series of incredible tragedies. Paraguay is completely flooded, the Iguasu waterfalls just disappeared last week, the city of Guadalajara exploded—several kilometers in a working class neighborhood, and L.A. was on fire. Our continent is going through tremendous pains. And certainly I feel that this is linked with this triple end, the end of the decade and the century and the millennium, and with the beginning of a new society.

Thompson: Do you feel that the new society is already here?

Gómez-Peña: Yes, I do.

Thompson: You do a piece in which you say "art nostalgia, quality control," and I wanted you to explain that.

Gómez-Peña: One of the things I am trying to investigate in my work is trans-culture, and what is happening to Latin American culture when it crosses the border, how the U.S. creates simulacra of authenticity, of Latin culture, how Latin America chooses through the departments of tourism and culture to broadcast itself to the outside. There is a text in this new performance, which I will call "The New World Border," that deals very much with this official trans-culture, or what I call Free Trade Art. This, or the amigoization of the North, this kind of phony Latino culture without thorns, without barbed wire, without viscera, without blood and saliva, this homogenized kind of Latino American culture that is crafted to appeal to the desire of American and European yuppies. It often gets mistaken for what otherwise would be the true cultural achievements of the Latin American population within the U.S., whereas in fact it is the opposite. It is coming from above, and it is programmed perfectly to offer a simulacrum of peaceful coexistence and racial harmony. I in fact propose as an antidote to this official trans-culture, to this simulacrum of Latin America, to these inflatable Fridas and chili capsules and holographic naked mariachis that I talk about, I oppose this other culture coming from within, from underneath, this culture coming from a grass-roots level, this culture produced by the various communities who act in friction with everyday reality. There are two sources of identity for us: one imposed by the state, and one coming from within—or multiple identities coming from within, and those are the ones that interest me more; they are much more fluid, open-ended, and they allow for hybrids, for transition, for multiplicity, for duality.

For example, there is a difference between the post-earthquake rock and roll produced by the youth of Mexico City, which is an attempt to chronicle the pain of the city after the earthquake, this culture of reconstruction...

Thompson: The same sort of thing will happen in Los Angeles...

Gómez-Peña: ...versus the Latino boom created by Broadway tycoons and Hollywood moguls. I think that we often tend to mistake one for the other, but they are very very different. I oppose the Northern model of multiculturalism, which is a Dantean model, the *flaneur* who descends to the South, who descends to hell, to Latin America, in search of enlightenment, and then comes back to present what he or she has discovered, versus the multiculturalism of the South, which takes power from the state. And although I oppose the Dantean model of multiculturalism, I subscribe totally to the other one, in the same way that I oppose marginality for us who have experienced it for five hundred years—whereas the dominant culture glorifies marginality because it's an act of privilege for a Western bohemian to be marginal, to live in a bad neighborhood, to hang out with the bad guys, to drink exotic substances, to not have access to the media, to not have a national voice....

Thompson: But they always have their American Express card in their pocket, they don't leave home without it.

Gómez-Peña: And for us marginality is a five-hundred-year-old reality, and in fact what we want is to speak from the center. That's why I think that it's important to not mistake these processes that many people often mistake. In the Chicano community, for example, unlike the Anglo-American community, when an artist begins to get some recognition, he is not distrusted. In New York, if an Anglo-American artist begins to get too much recognition, he is immediately distrusted, because he obviously sold out, he has become commercial, he is not esoteric enough. Whereas I just found out yesterday that my beloved compadre, Amalia Mesa-Bains just won a MacArthur, and that is going to be a fact of celebration for the entire Chicano community, because we don't get MacArthurs that often.

Thompson: You received that grant too. Were you expecting to win it? How have you accepted it, and how have your friends accepted it?

Gómez-Peña: I received it last year. I wasn't expecting it at all. And as I say, for the most part the alternative arts community, the chicano community, and all my artists of color colleagues, have celebrated with me very much, and I have felt incredible gratitude. But it has also created incredible distrust in the dominant community, because they are used to seeing chicanos as disempowered, they are used to seeing us as emerging voices—

Thompson: *Always* emerging.

Gómez-Peña: This is so they *can* discover us, so they have the privilege to discover us, you know? And when suddenly we are speaking from the center, with access to the media, and there is a symmetry, they immediately distrust us. They wish that Guillermo was ill, poor, and unknown, as I was a few years ago. But the good thing is that this has given me a little bit more negotiating power, which I can hopefully use to open doors for other colleagues. And it has given my words some extra weight, and I have to be particularly more careful and responsible for what I say, because that has put me in a position of leadership in the chicano community.

Thompson: Do you like that?

Gómez-Peña: Yes and no. Because especially in the last two years, since I received the Prix de la Parole in the International Theater Festival in Montréal the year before I received the MacArthur, my life has been completely scrutinized. My private life has become threatened. And even the tone of the media has changed. Before, they used to deal with the content of my work, and now they want to deal with personal issues, which is not good. This country has a serious problem in making a distinction between having fame and having a national voice, between the culture of hype and the culture of ideas, between being a public intellectual and being a celebrity. And it's very hard to remain in the territory of ideas and public dialogue, and not just to become an icon of Otherness, or a seasonal celebrity. One is constantly fighting for that, because what one wants to inhabit is a politicized intercultural space, and to use one's public voice to participate in the chronicling of contemporary America and the contemporary American crisis. What this country is undergoing right now is comparable to what many Latin American and African and Eastern European countries are undergoing. There is big trouble in America; there is an undeclared war taking place in the streets of America, and if we don't find very soon the models of peaceful co-existence and intercultural dialogue, we might end this century in a big racial war. I am extremely worried. I feel that what artists and intellectuals can offer is the creation of utopian models, but then the task is how to transfer these utopian models to the political arena, so they don't just remain within the confines of the artworld or the cultural institutions. I think Carlos Fuentes said it well: Our continent is inhabited by extremely imaginative artists and writers and extremely unimaginative politicians. He said that artists and writers have been developing incredible models of peaceful co-existence and cultural fusions, exchanges and dialogues, and yet these models have very rarely transferred to the political arena to create enlightened political systems that really speak to us as Americans in the widest sense of the term, as citizens of the Americas. But hopefully in the '90s we as artists can conquer more central spaces to speak from, and function as cross-cultural diplomats, as counter-journalists, as border pirates, as experimental activists.

Mildred Thompson *is a painter and sculptor who has exhibited widely in the United States, Europe, and Africa. This interview was originally part of a longer discussion between Thompson, Gómez-Peña, and Keith Antar Mason.*

2

Martha Rosler

Interviewed by Robert Fichter and Paul Rutkovsky

Martha Rosler is an artist, critic, and educator whose work in photography, performance, and video has been exhibited throughout the world, including the 1987 Whitney Biennial and Documenta 8. An associate professor at Rutgers University, her books include 3 Works *and* Service: A Trilogy on Colonization *(a collection of three postcard novels about food). In Rosler's 1973 performance (and videotape),* Vital Statistics of a Citizen, Simply Obtained *the artist undergoes procedures inspired by government photographs of women being measured; her work often examines the connections between documentary, bureaucracy, perception, and power. "The Bowery in Two Inadequate Descriptive Systems," in* 3 Works, *is a series of texts and photographs that "not only exposes the 'myths' of photographic objectivity and transparency; it also upsets the (modern) belief in vision as a privileged means of access to certainty and truth" (Craig Owens, "Feminists and Postmodernism"). More recently, Rosler organized the exhibition and book,* If You Lived Here, *both sponsored by the Dia Foundation, dealing exhaustively with the social issues and individual experiences faced by the homeless. She has been throughout her career a political artist, yet her work is without the overt harangue often associated with that term. She is an interventionist in both the social realm and the realm of art. The following conversation with artists Paul Rutkovsky and Robert Fichter took place in 1988.*

Robert Fichter: Why do you think the documentary should continue to exist?

Martha Rosler: That's a funny question, because I've written about documentaries as a dead form. But without some reference to the real, there's no place of departure.

Fichter: Do you think the documentary actually deals with the real?

Rosler: I think the documentary makes some effort to locate something outside subjectivity, even if it doesn't ever quite reach that point. It's like an asymptote, a point toward which it tends. The problem with classical documentary was that it acted as though you could stand totally outside your own self and just be the camera or be suspended outside time and space. There's a certain godlike, magical imaginary subject that drives classical, old-fashioned photography.

Paul Rutkovsky: Do you think it could ever be objective?

Rosler: No, I think that belief was very naive. But there is something to be salvaged there. To suggest that it can't be perfect is not to suggest that there was nothing to aim for. There is something to be aimed for, even if the strategies you end up with don't look too much like classical documentary. I still think the effort to represent the real, or at least to represent something beyond either complete interiority or complete surface, is essential. I think it's the basis for all representation.

Rutkovsky: What do you think representing the real is in the documentary?

Rosler: Well, I think it's a more rather than a less adequately complex account of meaning in the world, interpersonal and physical, social.

Rutkovsky: Do you think the documentary is important enough to continue within your work?

Rosler: I've never done anything that looks much like documentary, but I still take it as a base line. And although I've depended in many instances on the look of the hand-made, I've always used techniques of reproduction, often in contrast to the use of another, nonphotographic sign system. It isn't meant to be unmediated, only to suggest some evasion to the dictates of technology, not actually to evade them. I'm very suspicious of an effort to be too craft-oriented—I think that has been a trap, especially for women, because of the apparent naiveté and traditionalism involved. I prefer to refer to hand facture and even amateurishness rather than to do or be it.

What I'm doing now is hardly in the line of documentary, because what I've been interested in is the representations of representations, and in representations of things that reside in the public space, billboard images and television commercials. You might think of that as a documentary of signs in culture, but that is stretching the meaning of documentary past all usefulness.

Fichter: You make objects. What would you like those things to do?

Rosler: I'd like to provide some kind of critical distance, some kind of critical consciousness, so that when people come away from whatever it is I've done, they have some sense of a new apprehension of our own context, the possibility of a new view, or the wherewithal to make a judgment about meaning and value, and social responsibility. I'd like people to consider questions of their own power and ability to act on their own judgments about social organization and even about matters of empowerment between people, as well as on larger political issues.

Fichter: Do you feel videotape at this point is the quickest way to get the idea out to the most people?

Rosler: Video is particularly appealing to me because so many people know what it's all about—you know, it's television, it's an excellent place to start. Everyone knows the terms of address. And if what I'm actually presenting is somewhat apart from the normal, at least people have a basis of familiarity from which to depart. So I find video very helpful; also, I'm interested in it because it's still so technically poor. It very much has the look of a vernacular. It isn't frightening, and it isn't particularly arty— although in the hands of some people it is. But video offers a possibility of democratic use of this technology.

Rutkovsky: You don't see that happening necessarily?

Rosler: Young people are using video technology, but by and large they're doing imitations of MTV. That's inevitable, but I wish they would move away from outright copying. Still, the more independent video they see, the more chance they'll do something different.

Rutkovsky: Do you have hope?

Rosler: I'm not looking for utopia. I think you work with the means that are available. If it becomes impossible to use them meaningfully later, then it's probably time to move on to something else.

Rutkovsky: In Iran, the medium was the audiotape, and there are times when the media can mobilize the culture into action. It seems to me that our culture has so much "give" to it at the moment, that there's little room for real action.

Rosler: You mean, I think, that there's so much room for things to be encompassed by the culture that it's like elastic. Whereas in Iran everything was locked up tight, repressive and authoritarian, so any movement away from officially controlled culture was a revolutionary move.

The idea of a culture with a lot of give that's able to defuse dissension by allowing it to occur is similar to Herbert Marcuse's notion of repressive tolerance: that all kinds of representations, by being tolerated, are rendered harmless. Also, we're a much more media-sophisticated culture than Iran...But looked at in terms of the media that are used to channel dissent, if nonbroadcast video were to be banned here tomorrow, then videotapes would probably become an active revolutionary tool, just as plain old photocopy became a subversive channel in the Soviet Union.

Rutkovsky: I wonder if there is potentially anything that might replace the videotape and photocopy and be more accessible? Some of us thought the computer would be a powerhouse of information that almost anyone could manipulate and take control of. That does not seem to be happening.

Rosler: Are we making the mistake of getting stuck in a particular means of production, rather than looking at the types of messages propagated on it? To make an audiotape in Iran meant to make an audiotape of the Ayatollahs, not just any audiotape. It was the institutional context of those audiotapes as representatives of a repressed religious tradition that gave them power. Just as it's not xeroxed copies of Pravda but xeroxed copies of *Samizdat* literature that became powerful in the Soviet Union. So it isn't the computer per se, but the suggestion that the computer would have allowed the organization and dissemination of genuinely subversive material. I guess what I'm trying to say is that in this culture there is very little that can be perceived as subversive in any fundamental sense because most things are allowed into expression. What isn't "allowed" is direct political expression, at least of the left half of the spectrum, in mainstream contexts, and what's most interesting is that it's not repressed or censored, it's erased. For example, consider that the mildest form of centrist liberalism is referred to in this country as "left," or even as "extreme left" or "radical"! Everything that might lead to the expression of politically focused dissidence is forbidden or erased in advance. So, you wind up with a kind of self-erasing collective memory, and people, including and especially those who work in the news media, constantly engage in self-censorship.

Fichter: Can you give an example of that?

Rosler: It pervades all of the news media, at every moment. Although this country offers its citizens very little news indeed of the rest of the world—except about strategic political situations—we are constantly congratulating ourselves on being the best informed society in the history of the world. We may be the best entertained, but we certainly are very poorly informed. Spend a couple of weeks in Canada, say, or anywhere else in the Western world, to observe the contrast in what gets reported, and how. Everything we hear of is reported from the point of view of our political/military interests. Witness the rank distortion of news about Nicaragua [during the Sandinista era], a country referred to constantly in the context of "Cuba and the Soviet Union," as though that defined its existence. It is depicted as a communist dictatorship, although more than half its businesses are privately owned and its leadership was popularly elected in what was acknowledged around the world to be the fairest election in Central America.

But to offer an entirely different kind of erasure: When I was a graduate student in the early '70s in San Diego, there was a very active group called the Women's Liberation Front, whose membership included women from on and off campus. It founded the pioneering daycare center on campus, which still exists, withstanding several efforts by the administration to close it. When I was teaching there last year, there was a very disingenuous effort on the part of a former chancellor, who had gone on to bigger and better things, to present his view of that campus in the late '60s and early '70s, one that was a very significant distortion of the actual events. I avoided these talks, not wanting to suffer raised blood pressure. A number of activists from that period, who were still around, challenged the former chancellor and subsequently held a couple of talks on the real nature and context of the political organizing of that period. But a number of my women students reported, with great perturbation, that the guys giving the talk forgot to mention the Women's Liberation Front. When challenged, they admitted they'd forgotten all about the group and about its founding of the women's center and the daycare center. I told the women students that I still had position papers and organizing leaflets back in New York from that period, and I subsequently sent them copies.

My point is that even on the left itself, an extraordinarily important organizing force on a University of California campus, a group that was a full-fledged member and constant presence in the antiwar coalition was gone from collective memory. A few people like me who happened to save printed material could substantiate a different account.... I think that as a society we engage in this kind of collective delusion about the shape of the past. Another sort of example might be the current elevation of the Beatles to being the pre-eminent, almost the only, musical expression of the '60s, because, in many ways, they were the least threatening—thereby demoting not only the Rolling Stones, but Dylan, Joan Baez, Janis Joplin, Jimi Hendrix, Jefferson Airplane, Country Joe and the Fish, Motown, Eric Clapton, Cream, and even the Dave Clark Five, to mention just a few. The more technologically dependent our culture becomes, the more we seem to pretend that the past is different from what it was—and from what it was recorded to be. We seem to have given over the powers of memory, the lifeline of any culture, to our machinery. Yet we seem also to have collectively agreed never to review the data without some bizarre acts of selective reinterpretation—standing meaning on its head, as some people are trying to do now about Vietnam. So, in some ways, I suppose, I'm pessimistic.

Our collective forgetting makes the organizing of alternative cultures something that has to be reinvented every ten years. But, on the other hand, there are people who pass along history in an oral tradition, and this too is periodically rediscovered—though efforts to make use of this populist resource lost out when they were targeted for defunding under the Reagan Administration's control of the National Endowment for the Humanities. Still, in the mainstream media there's so much data collected that sorting through them is a staggering job, perhaps too staggering.

Rutkovsky: That troubles me.

Rosler: But we really can't expect a machine to be the archivist, as well as the archive! We can't rely on technology to do the sorting, people have to do it....

Fichter: So what you're suggesting is that we have to train a new generation of technics or media conscious....

Rosler: I'd say activists, people to be active in relation to whatever medium it is and to whatever social practice it is. In other words, not necessarily political activists but social activists. I think that's essential. The problem is, I think, that if you train people as a technical, they'll behave like a technical elite. I'm interested in retaining some aspect of the guerrilla—if you'll pardon the romanticism. You know, somebody interested in rubbing the social fur the wrong way. Someone with a critical consciousness. Someone who says, "O.K., I know your rules, I wonder if we won't get farther by bending them?" But not just for the sake of breakage....

I think that it's very necessary for me, as an art maker, constantly to make the point that art is about private experience in the context of a world made up of other people. It isn't about private experience as a value in and of itself. I think it's important to see art not just as a holding action in which the private self is maintained against the bureaucratic world, but as one in which the public world needs to be rescued along with that sense of self, as the medium of experience.

Rutkovsky: Do you consciously avoid the art world?

Rosler: Yes...and no. It's no secret that the art world is currently market driven. You know, I sound like an old fart; it's too bad that I happen to be moving into old farthood just when it's the young who have become terribly cynical—and that, for many, that's what keeps their art going—or so they claim. It's not, perhaps, a real cynicism, it's a quoted cynicism, the alienation of bohemia. Still, there's no question that the art world is the major receiving ground of my work, and I'd be foolish to pretend otherwise.

I don't intend to "abandon" the art world. I don't want to jump ship. But I don't want to be rocked by every swell and undertow, and I don't intend to follow the fads. There's a point when you've decided who you are, and you don't want to put on a new skin or a new mask every week. That's only normal. But I do find this to be a particularly uninteresting moment—it has been since Ronald Reagan was elected. From my point of view, the changes in the art world are a predictable response of capital to crisis: the return to the forefront of public attention of money and of status based on money. Of course, this would take place in an area with a highly valued symbolism, that is, the art world. You would have to be blinkered not to see how the art world has changed, and the art world rhetoric has changed, at the same time that the rhetoric of the public world changed, both away from a kind of populism and even egalitarian pluralism, around 1980.

Rutkovsky: Do you see yourself stepping around the periphery of the art world—jumping?

Rosler: Jumping from ice floe to ice floe.... We ought to be careful about these romanticized images, but there's something to it! The sense of precariousness, and a kind of discomfort with the grounding the art world offers, the perception of it as a series of shoals waiting to dump some poor artist under—especially in my case, since my art has an element of unlovability. When I find particular works are becoming loved, I figure they've outlived their time.

Rutkovsky: Like the Bowery piece for instance?

Rosler: I'm thinking more of certain videotapes that have become popular for museums to collect right now. It makes me nervous. In some ways I've been historicized, and school libraries, for instance, seem to be buying some works for their place in the past. Which means that their interest is not so uncomfortable that they would have trouble seeing the work as some kind of framed and aestheticized object, an entity created to make them feel good. That whole axis of meaning is one that I don't want to be stuck on.

Robert Fichter is an artist who teaches in the Department of Art at Florida State University; Paul Rutkovsky, also an artist, is associate professor of art at Florida State University and a fellow of the Center for Advanced Visual Studies, M.I.T.

3

Group Material

Interviewed by Critical Art Ensemble

Group Material is an artists' collective that was founded in 1979, when the group opened one of the first storefront artspaces in the Lower East Side of Manhattan. There they organized a series of exhibitions that embraced neighborhood concerns and challenged the surrounding mercantile culture. As the group evolved, the storefront was abandoned for more public sites, and the membership dropped from twelve to four. The four who remained were Doug Ashford, Julie Ault, Mundy McLaughlin, and Tim Rollins. From 1981 to 1987, Group Material sought to present the art community and the general public with political information through art by re-presenting the works of other artists in carefully orchestrated thematic group shows, or through the collection and presentation of information and artifacts from local and nonart communities. By 1987, Mundy McLaughlin and Tim Rollins had left and Félix González-Torres had joined the group.

Group Material's exhibitions have included DA ZI BAOS, *a public installation on Union Square, March 1983;* Timeline: A Chronicle of U.S. Intervention in Central and Latin America, *January 1984 (organized for Artists Call);* Americana, *March 1985 (organized for the Whitney Biennial); and more recently* Democracy, *the 1990 project that was in progress when this interview was conducted. Democracy was sponsored by the Dia Foundation, and included an exhibition, town meetings, and a book. Since this 1988 interview,* Group Material *has been less active as an collective than as individual artists, though some activities were under their collaborative name through 1996.*

Group Material: I would be lying if I told you that GM wanted to exist totally outside the systematic contradictions of the "art-world." We entertain the idea of galleries; we entertain the idea of critics and taste. To do otherwise is symbolic self-censorship.

Critical Art Ensemble: Existing outside a system isn't possible anyway. The gallery system is the infrastructure of the art community. It can't be ignored.

GM: The real irony is that many oppositional stances to a system seem as much a part of it as anything else. Like the whole idea of the alternative space. It's as if these spaces have a guaranteed separation from a commercial order, when in fact they are often the proving grounds for commercialism. This is not an automatically bad thing, of course. I mean, I try to promote work I think is important whenever I can.

CAE: Why did Tim Rollins leave Group Material just as the press began to focus on him as a pivotal person in the group?

GM: We all have jobs and our own art practice. At this point, certain levels of production and effect for Tim and KOS now have the potential of happening. For him not to take advantage of this would be foolish. For others to criticize this careerism would be too easy.

CAE: The journals and the marketplace were looking for a dominant signature, and Tim's was the signature that became associated with GM. Was Tim leaving as a reaction against this market misrepresentation?

GM: No. There have always been misrepresentations. Part of it has been because of our own sloppiness and part because of how people are—people like the signature and it's hard for them to look at collaborations. Of course the failure of many writers to comprehend our project is predictable—but if we are going to judge our culture only through *Artforum* then we deserve the culture we get. If you want to pick on how GM has been misrepresented, as with the treatment of Tim, you should also ask about all the other ways it has been misrepresented.

CAE: Such as?

GM: That we are all curators. We are not curators, we are artists who are re-presenting, re-presenting other people's work, in a context that is making "another statement," "a piece." Another misunderstanding is that it's all pedagogical. That went on for a while. That has chilled out, but the belief continued for a while that we are all teachers, and that GM was involved in some kind of educational research. Two of the members of GM were not teachers. This is like saying we're doing psychic research, because one of our members happens to do readings for people on a professional basis.

CAE: Is there anything else you want to say about the disadvantages or advantages of the use of collaboration, as compared to more mainstream styles of art production?

GM: Well, this might sound a little bizarre, but I really don't believe that anyone today is working alone with his muse in the garret. I don't think it's possible any more. (I do think that some people *believe* that they are working in a purely personal and special way.) Information—and don't we all know this yet?—has taken on a universal level where you aren't working by yourself, in the same sense that you can't think politically by yourself. You can't not pay your taxes, you can't not have a checkbook. You can't not have a social security number. Welcome to modernity.

CAE: So your basic assumption is that art is a social institution that can only function within a social milieu.

GM: Yes, I've always assumed that's a given.

CAE: Is the collective method on the rise?

GM: To collaborate isn't enough. Our proposal wasn't that we would necessarily change the relationship between audience and author just by saying, "We're not an individual artist." We wanted to truly affect the social relations that surround the production and distribution of artwork. I still have questions about the consistency seen in much of the other collaborative work that is around. It's like the methodology is hidden. If GM chose this strategy I don't think you would have gotten the variety of that certain thematic involvement with the world; I don't think you would have gotten as many different positions and different involvements with different sorts of political and cultural groups within any one exhibition. But it is really the nature of our product that sets us apart.

CAE: But that is why a collective is necessary. A person can only specialize, speak, or produce in a limited number of realms with any authority. After that you have to rely on other specialized backup.

GM: My problem with this is that even though I know that a lot of GM's uniqueness is due to the collective method, I don't want to stress method over product. GM has always tried to inform its projects with the expertise and voices of others.

CAE: What do you think about specificity in political art?

GM: A lot of political art does the same thing with content that expressionist art does with emotion. That is, it takes this issue and says, "I'm going to paint some dripping red letters, and some screaming children and then I'm going to be a political artist." In contrast, what GM has been trying to do is diagram different social forces, such as in the show *Timeline,* which was informed by working with the Committee of International Solidarity of the People of El Salvador, Taller Latinoamericano, Casa Nicaragua, and others who brought information from sources radically different from the dominant media. Without them and chance meetings with artists and intellectuals who were here in exile from Central America, our work wouldn't have been possible.

Actually, our relationship with these groups began two years earlier with a show called *Luchar.* There were things in that show from Mexico City, from Salvador, from Managua, that we displayed next to Leon Golub, Martha Rosler, Mike Glier, etc. The opening turned into a kind of mass meeting between artists and activists. There were speeches by Lucy Lippard and the NYC representative of the FDR/FMLN. An organization of El Salvadoran artists and intellectuals was founded. There was a kind of reciprocity, with people's agendas informing various artistic practice and the art exhibition becoming the springboard for political organization. And it didn't end there; two years later we saw Artist's Call Against U.S. Intervention in

Central America organize cultural professionals as a group around this issue, to actually affect our industry in North and Central America.

CAE: What is the artist's responsibility to the community?

GM: Our exhibitions and projects gather different levels of cultural production into one site. By doing this we are automatically serving more artists and audiences than the mainstream. A lot of specific shows have had specific community concerns; a lot of them touch social relationships in the way the artwork is perceived. In other words, why can't an art show be organized that has a different level of concern besides the specialized artist? A show like *People's Choice*, which was an exhibition of artworks and artifacts in the early GM space, was obviously working out of a concern for the neighborhood of the exhibition space rather than for art-trained professionals.

CAE: Did you have good community turnout for *People's Choice*?

GM: Well, remember the entire show was made up of objects collected from the block. GM went door to door asking people for their most beautiful paintings, their most important pictures. (This was before my time—I was still a student and part of GM's enthusiastic audience.) It was obvious to everyone that *People's Choice* was the most important show that the group did during that period, because it totally transformed the supposedly neutral gallery into an icon of the neighborhood. The show wasn't based on what the "experts" thought best represented the neighborhood; these objects were what the people on the block valued as beautiful.

Back to our conversation about specialists: you see, merely collaborating with others will not confront the destructive nature of privatized culture. The specialist might be the very audience that for so long has been locked out of the industry. In *Luchar,* the specialist might be the designer making posters in Salvador literally on the front—whose life depends on it.

CAE: When you did the subway piece did you ride on the subway and see what the response was? Were people just reading their *Daily News* or actually paying attention and reading the GM pieces?

GM: We chose those particular ads in the subway, just above eye level, because people really do read them. If you get on and it's crowded, you can't read the paper. There's also the "don't look at me and I won't look at you" routine on the subway already. In that kind of social space, you look up—where *Subculture* was installed. At that time the subway was a radical site for the installation of "public" art. Later it became standard institutional fare.

CAE: Was it part of the agenda for *Subculture* and *DA ZI BAOS* to disrupt everyday life structure?

GM: No. I don't think that it's necessarily any more of a disruption than the normal level of media onslaught that we have to live with. The idea with *Subculture* was that through some level of collectivization, the pooling of resources, any individual can intercept that onslaught, can participate relatively; it was no big financial deal because each artist in the show covered the costs of producing a series of images. We paid the installation fee and dealt with bureaucrats.

CAE: Wouldn't such installations necessarily have an alienating effect since you're breaking habituation? What you put on the subway wasn't a hemorrhoid ad.

GM: Some work mimicked the advertising almost to the letter, and I'm sure that it was read with the same sort of psychotic level of consumption that just goes through you. But my feeling still is that some of the most successful work was the painting, because painting in that context was really shocking. An artist named Merrie Dee did twenty-seven identical paintings of a woman running from a burning shack in the middle of a field. It was a learning experience for me—here we were really talking up the authority of graphic forms and asking everyone to keep in mind the corporate aesthetic and content of most subway advertising—and when we got it all up on the trains...the paintings in many ways were the most dangerous.

CAE: Do you find that shows work better outdoors, where you make the first move to engage the audience, with perhaps *People's Choice* notwithstanding?

GM: Let's remember that just because art is placed outdoors, that doesn't make it public. Group Material has tried to approach the relationship between artists and audiences on two levels, among others. Some projects have enlarged the capacity that the gallery has to represent different aesthetic agendas— *People's Choice* was an example, but so is *Americana*. By exhibiting household appliances at the Whitney Museum we were pointing out that curators aren't the only people that make aesthetic choices. Other projects have tried to expose these agendas to other artists: in *Subculture* we asked "What kind of work would you make for a subway?" and in *Timeline* we asked, "What kind of work would you make to chronicle our government's military intervention?"

CAE: Is GM going to take these shows out of urban areas, and thereby change the context in which they are presented even more?

GM: The *DA ZI BAOS* project, where we interviewed institutions and individuals and compared them at a public level on large-scale poster work, should be done across the country. We have done it in Wales because we were invited to do it by an organization there. I would love that every time we go someplace to produce *DA ZI BAOS* in response to local issues. It still is planned to do this at nuclear dump sites in a place like Montana or New Hampshire—one of those rural towns where sixty percent of the people are unemployed and a local government can say, "All right, we'll dump here, and we'll all get jobs and the city will garner a lot of tax revenue." Of course, not everyone says yes. What these issues produce is often a level of participatory democracy that is at best rare in urban politics. The town meeting, for Group Material, is a particularly relevant cultural process. And it's fascinating how this American institution, this tradition, can be paralleled with a project modeled after the *DA ZI BAOS* (large character posters) of China's cultural revolution.

There is something here about GM's project that I think should be mentioned, because it's important to understand in taking on this kind of work. That is, try not to become satisfied with the opportunities and offers. Throughout the life of the group we've tried to balance invitations with self-initiated works like *DA ZI BAOS*. One has to remember that any agency, not just the patron, can become an ideological taskmaster. And meanwhile, the mayor of Anytown isn't on the phone as we speak, ready to say, "We really like you guys. Why don't you come over and hook up one of those *DA ZI BAOS* for us?"

You should do Documenta. You should do the Whitney Museum—not only for their audiences but to reach a level of institutional notice that helps to develop other audiences. Barbara Kruger has been saying this for years and recently has been attacked for her "commercialism." But Barbara's billboards are up in little towns across the country. *We Don't Need Another Hero* was up in Philmont, New York, the home of Oliver North. It wouldn't have happened if she had decided to resign herself to some naive idealist idea of populist art that rejected every capitalist organ of production.

CAE: We've touched on theory, so while we're on this subject, let me ask you about *Resistance (Anti-Baudrillard)*. Why did GM feel so strongly about the use of Baudrillard's theory that you had a show against him? And how much of it was homage to him?

GM: It was not an homage; it was not against him. What GM wanted to do was to take the Baudrillard we had used in the past, the Baudrillard of *The Mirror of Production* and *Critique of the Political Economy of the Sign,* and compare him to the art-world's love image that was so apparent at that time. *Resistance* wasn't about Baudrillard the person or even directly about his writings for that matter. It was about how critical factors in our industry become complicit with status quo visions of culture and history—a complicity I think we all experience. Even Baudrillard himself got up in public to declare, "This is not about art." What we were interested in with *Resistance* was how a contestational theory was being used and abused, and to question that use through the exhibition of different kinds of artifacts. We grounded the whole exhibition on video. We had three monitors that were to act as a triumvirate ground of how media gets sublimated. The objects in the show covered a spectrum of oppositional strategies artists can adopt—from producing graphics for SWAPO (the Southwest African People's Organisation) or local New York labor unions to making work in the gallery like Mike Glier, Hans Haacke, Nancy Spero. Also, we tried to show historical precedent for this kind of process: Heartfield in terms of the activist, Redon in terms of the dream, Catherine Allport in terms of photojournalism. You see, if Ashley Bickerton is suddenly proclaimed a "contestational" artist then what kind of artists are in Guerilla Art Action Group?

CAE: So it seems that you were much more worried about (at least at that point) the massive proliferation of simulationist art that was all grounding itself in a misrepresentation of Baudrillard's theories, rather than in Baudrillard's theories themselves.

GM: Yes, that's it but—well, look, there are massive holes in the later work. If social science *is* science fiction, then that means that all the work in the simulationist program is what all the academics (who are eating the shit up) say it is. But I don't think that Baudrillard is right, and my students at Bedford-Stuyvesant don't think he's right, and eighty percent of the people who have ever struggled to try and change the fuckedupness of this world don't think he's right. I'm pretty convinced that using a theoretical model based entirely on language is a mistake. As artists, we leave the social relations and social determination out of this again and again.

CAE: So are we back to the Critical Theory school?

GM: Not necessarily. Although a re-reading now and then couldn't hurt. Let's use post-structuralism as a tool, use it as a way of deciphering things and stories, in a way that might expose the social forces that lead to the inability to read in the first place. Why this author? Why this meal? Why this kind of coffee? Let's use Barthes to find out how the world is built as a series of mythologies, but then try to find out why these mythologies were built and maybe more important—who built them.

CAE: Do you think that the GM *Resistance* show did counter the practice to some degree and change the use of Baudrillard by the New York art community?

GM: Other things happened that make it OK now to say "I hate Baudrillard," but it certainly wasn't because of us. Even though GM is committed to practical models—to actually doing things—we're not anti-theory. Let's not feed the traditional delusionary practices that avoid theoretical contradiction. Dripping red letters are not working.

Recently, in the past four or five years, there has been a lot of writing around the idea of a resistant postmodernism. This work, even if outlining an excellent theoretical program, continues to ignore many of the practical models that surround it. There is a whole terrain of cultural production—collaborative, community-based, pedagogical, or just plain subcultural processes—that won't fit into the "fine art" category. Here I might sound like a traditional Marxist, but I feel that the reason these models are ignored has to do with class comfort with risky theory over resistant practice.

CAE: It seems that you see the theory-praxis problem as completely unresolved, despite all the rhetoric of the French Marxists that theory is praxis. Do you still have questions about the problem?

GM: In our industry it's certainly a mess. I mean, we both know how rare it is to read something that can both reflect the sense of beauty and the history that one can find in an art object or other cultural moment. Recently, GM has tried to have writers who usually address other disciplines and audiences become involved with our project. For *Constitution* we published essays by Judge Bruce Wright, a federal judge in New York, and Michael and Margie Ratner, from the Center for Constitutional Rights. We really wanted to supply something a little more useful than the usual promotional stuff. We all have to remember that the specialized art community, as an intellectual sphere, is a very unusual place and always has been.

CAE: At least since the nineteenth century.

GM: It's been a site of relatively incredible intellectual mobility, a minefield of cultural production, half brilliant and half shit, but nonetheless creating a discourse and an audience for ideas that other fields rarely match. Or look at Artists Call Against U. S. Intervention in Central America—it was able to use the whole institutional framework of the artworld to raise money on a totally practical level. Here was a group, of maybe fifteen or twenty in New York, using the market structure to do real political work. Real resources were raised for real struggles.

CAE: What are the information options for those not wanting to read theory?

GM: Well, let's take this supposedly theoretical idea of "appropriation." With the high school kids that I teach, there is an intrinsic knowledge about appropriation, because for them in a sense, all cultural production has to be stolen. White culture historically never let you proclaim the culture that you had. It's not talked about, it's not taught, it's not on TV. And even within a group of young artists—for graffiti writers, to bite something and make it your own is a sign of greatness. Tap dancers build whole repertoires of stolen steps. There's the idea within folk culture of how imagery gets communicated, appropriated, and turned into new imagery.

CAE: Tell us about the *Inserts* project that you tried to get in the New York *Daily News* just recently.

GM: It's not unlike *Subculture,* our project for the subway. Group Material feels that these huge organs of the advertising world should be approached for disseminating work. *Inserts* will be a twelve-page advertising supplement to the Sunday paper containing ten artists' works developed specifically for this context. It will reach about 200,000 readers in various neighborhoods of the city. This time I feel we're really building a bridge between public funding and a program of dissemination that actually reaches people. Public agencies don't have to limit themselves to supporting the same old pedestrian blockers, lobby fillers, or museum blockbusters. I understand from talking to Jenny Holzer that a lot of TV channels will sell late night ad spots for peanuts. Can you imagine the audience?

CAE: So it's the audience size that interests you the most in using this medium?

GM: The size, and the method of address. There are all these resources being spent on the reproduction of artwork—why not make a catalog that exists in the public sphere instead of in the alternative art space?

CAE: What can we expect in the future from GM?

GM: We're working on a project called "Democracy" that will take place at the Dia Art Foundation next fall and winter. It will be a five-month series of exhibitions and meetings that will examine the current crisis in American democracy. In a way this is a dream come true—a chance to rigorously involve other voices in our working process. You see, as great as I feel GM's contribution so far has been—it usually has been a spectacle of relations between different communities. In other words, just because you show a Thomas Lawson painting next to graphics from the Redistribute America Movement doesn't mean that these two kinds of producers develop any working influence, or even acknowledgment for that matter. Of course it happens—but the exhibition in itself remains a model of possibilities instead of actual organizing tools. This is a goal.

Anyway, with "Democracy" we've planned a series of round-table discussions with artists, critics, policymakers, and theorists, that will both inform the exhibition and establish agendas for public town meetings coinciding with the show. We're trying to replace the traditional lecture/panel method of presenting information with a more public method. Each show will be surrounded by the social forces that make art possible in the first place and each discourse will be exemplified by the cultural work it implies. A book documenting this whole process will be distributed by Dia afterwards.

To me, what's really important is how all this is going to affect history. I don't mean to sound egotistical about it, but ten years after witnessing the beginnings of GM as a member of the audience, I'm finally realizing that it's possible to have an effect on things. It's shocking; sometimes even embarrassing. But now it's crucial that we have control over how our project is represented and stop being distorted by magazine interpreters who just need the fucking copy. Or...I don't know what they need—copy, fashion, theory? So anyway, "Democracy" is a dream of taking the spectacle of the exhibition and turning it into a series of social elevations. Turning it into a situation.

This interview was conducted by **Steve Kurtz** *of Critical Art Ensemble, which was formed in Tallahassee, Florida, in 1987 and is made up of six artists (Steve Kurtz, George Barker, Claudia Bucher, Steve Barnes, Dorian Burr, and Hope Kurtz).*

4

Tim Miller

Interviewed by Linda Frye Burnham

Tim Miller's work has always been autobiographical, a mixture of humor, monologue, and movement that charts a young man's voyage through the minefield that is gay cultural identity in this country. A Los Angeles native, he moved to New York at twenty-one and helped found Performance Space 122 in the East Village. Miller joined ACT UP (AIDS Coalition to Unleash Power) when it began in New York and continued as an active member when he moved to Los Angeles in the late '80s. Part of the great strength of ACT UP is its contingent of artists who create graphics, photographs, videos, and performances for public demonstrations. Miller created a manifesto for a week-long demonstration at L.A. County General Hospital, and was arrested with eighty-four other activists in 1989 for blocking the Federal Building in Westwood. Miller was also one of the "NEA 4," four performance artists whose grants were rescinded by then National Endowment for the Arts chairman John Frohnmeyer in the aftermath of the controversy over arts funding sparked by Andres Serrano's work (a 1990 interview with Serrano is included in this volume). The grants, to Miller, Karen Finley (also interviewed in this volume), Holly Hughes, and John Fleck were ultimately restored in a legal settlement. Miller's performances are an indissoluble combination of political intervention and provocational stage performance. This conversation with artist and writer Linda Burnham took place in 1990, just as the NEA crisis was heating up.

Linda Burnham: What does a crisis like AIDS do to an artist's life?

Tim Miller: Obviously it connects you deeply with the reality of the world, the planet, fate, ultimate destiny. It cuts a lot of bullshit out, cuts a lot of competitive stupid stuff that can tend to dominate the art world or any world when it's not in a crisis. It decentralizes the artist's life. We talk about this endlessly: the artist-as-citizen issue where your time as a creative artist—which is still really special, like little precious jewels—goes to organizing efforts and political activities. Before, there was this great romantic split between making a living and making your art. And now it's like—who cares about that? Everybody's got to make a living and we'll do that one way or another. The real thing is how much energy can keep your work going, keep trying to save the world and creating structures that encourage other artists to work and to be activated as well.

Burnham: Do you find yourself less or more able to focus on your artwork?

Miller: That decentralizing thing is really freeing. You stop being this neurotic creature that's worried about your every mood or anxiety spell. It means you have an impossible amount of work to do, especially trying to find some way of being creative within that; it's hopeless but you just sort of do your best and get through each day's tasks. What is writer's block within this kind of context? All that kind of psychologizing about creative process still exists, but you start getting creative inspiration in other places that are less about your blood sugar and more about being in intense situations that challenge you, that manifest your relationship to the state. A lot of people have laid aside their cultural upbringing within a bourgeois European avant-garde tradition, and their self-image, for other kinds of activity.

Burnham: Do you think that the last ten years have brought you any closer to the sense of what the artist's function really is in humankind?

Miller: This is the good question. That's where the idea of making work for demonstrations and the intensity of that life situation is so important. It brings up the image of entertaining the troops, like Bob Hope in Vietnam, God forbid. But in a way that's your most useful self. Like I say in the manifesto—

the cultural building block of having to inspire, warn, comfort each other around the feeble glow of the fire, as opposed to this fabulous, money-laden, chic theater kind of thing. Most of the work you and I are interested in is basically all about trying to make sense of things around a modest campfire or some kind of small light—in the sense of "the wolves are out there."

Burnham: What's a good example of artists doing that?

Miller: Well, there's no illusion of enormous power and prestige and empire around L.A.P.D. (Los Angeles Poverty Department, John Malpede's performance troupe of artists and homeless people). It's a much rawer and human kind of building block that derives its power and beauty from something besides international hip. That's a big change I think. It makes artists more interesting and stronger—probably who most of them want to be and why they wanted to become artists anyway, to help and to explore things, the things that really upset you. Long before I had any sense of art issues, I had a sense of injustice, of the world of unfairness. Maybe, to be quite honest, what precedes that is a sense of otherness, which all artists, certainly all gay artists, feel. But after that, the strongest emotional and intellectual challenges were about the world. It was the ultimate challenge and task *to see that it exists*, after growing up in middle-class Southern California, the great dissonance of that, and then taking it into writing and organizing, but especially into the work itself.

Burnham: I'd like to get to the particular character of ACT UP and ACT UP/LA. There's been criticism of the organization because it is so radical and outspoken. What attracts you to the combative style, for instance, the incidents of heckling politicians who take a friendly stance but are too soft in general, and the constant exposition of how little politicians are doing and the statements against working inside the system?

Miller: The great thing about all those things is they are so consistent with the history of the avant-garde, of shocking the bourgeoisie. Except now you actually do it, you don't pretend to do it by being in coffeehouses. You actually go to the halls of justice and law and power and confront them on their turf.

Burnham: You're actually confronting the structure of the establishment, the things that hold it up.

Miller: So that whole idea of "oh, you're just a crazy artist and you're critical of everything" (that being just a sort of neurotic or ingrown position) becomes a really outgoing and directed kind of response. It's all pure performance—challenging, exposing dishonesty and lies and contradictions.

Burnham: What changes have you seen in ACT UP in Los Angeles?

Miller: L.A. has gone through a very complicated peacemaking between the most activist-oriented and the more administrative-oriented. What happened in L.A. at the Federal Building has not happened in any other city in this country where the major bureaucracies line up with ACT UP on civil disobedience. That's never happened in New York.

Burnham: The major bureaucracies?

Miller: The major organizations: the head of AIDS Project L.A., Being Alive, The Gay Community Center, Minority AIDS Project, Cara a Cara. Also, that was a very mixed race, straight/gay, male/female, worker bee/executive director kind of event. It's what was most important about it. Very important things are going to come out of that for this community, which is the biggest, richest, and most organized gay community in this country. It's always been hyper-organized. It was the first Gay Community Center.

Burnham: What has been the most interesting action you've taken part in?

Miller: The real departure point in terms of L.A. and in another sense for me as an artist, the hospital vigil, was the most important thing that's happened so far because it was about the creation of an alternative space. I think the two most important alternative spaces that have happened this year in L.A. were Highways Performance Space and the vigil, because the vigil was also a cultural event, it was a performance space, it was happening every day—music, poetry, dance, performance art—and that's a very useful model for a lot of the things we're talking about. The artist becomes really woven into the community as a worker. Everybody talks about being a "cultural worker," but I think people are really starting to realize what that means, people are living it. John Malpede's definitely a cultural worker.

Burnham: It means putting in the hours, nine to five and longer.

Miller: And most of it is work, not writing sonnets. The work also happens to be highly creative and makes for really interesting art. When the art finally does happen it comes forward intimately woven into life and community, whether it's the way the dozens of people like myself who are artists, but also really involved in AIDS activism—in a way that changes the image you have of yourself in the world and what you do and your sense of service and being connected. The other thing that was really important about that as a model, is that it had tangible success—the AIDS ward exists. It was the beginnings of a more culturally diverse movement that has really come to fruition; people are beginning to know how to deal with each other. Major healing has gone on between gay Latinos and Anglo-Europeans.

Burnham: Because of ACT UP?

Miller: It's helped a lot, because people have been ready to go into conflict with each other and are ready to not write each other off on both sides.

Burnham: One of the things we brought up when we did our AIDS panel at HIGHWAYS was the impulse toward activism that's come out of the AIDS situation. And I don't mean political activism—I mean you get an idea and you do it, instead of letting it sit there on the table, because you might not be here tomorrow. So things have sort of speeded up because of this. I feel we can link that with the ACT UP "zap" philosophy—you know, do it now, do it quick, strike while the iron is hot.

Miller: Right, which is also ideally connected to the whole reason for being an artist in this particular realm (performance), which is to respond quickly, effectively, and surgically to what you want to do. I really see this with Guillermo Gómez-Peña. It's like a ray gun. He's going zzzz-t. It's very specific. There is no other art form or cultural way he could get at that, he couldn't make a movie about something that specific, he couldn't write a novel about it, but he could prepare a text, something he wrote that morning, and present it for public absorption that evening.

Burnham: It's related most closely to the way poetry functions politically in Latin American countries, I would guess.

Miller: My first impulse with performance, the reason I liked it, was because it was quick, it's still the reason I like it.

Burnham: You're not required to come up with three acts and scenery—

Miller: You don't show anybody a script—

Burnham: You don't really need any money—

Miller: You just do it. And that's probably why ACT UP and those strategies appeal so much to a certain kind of artist. This artist is intuitive, wants to move quickly, doesn't want to be bogged down in bureaucracy or over-discussing, and just wants to do things that are grounded in process, as every artist's quick decisions are. And ACT UP is most successful in its ability to quickly respond.

Burnham: There's another whole strain that's interesting to talk about too. Richard Schechner said at a conference last year that he felt that performance outside of the gallery or theater, in the street essentially, was extremely influenced by the civil rights demonstrations in the South—that watching the strategies of black activists at sit-ins and marches gave a formal impulse for artists to get out in the street, not necessarily to affect things politically, but just because they saw and fell in love with the power of the moving image in the context of everyday life.

Miller: Yes, I think that's the most recent example. But it goes so much further back. Look at all the great romantic French paintings of the students in the streets and the triumph of liberty and storming the barricades.

Burnham: Yes, but I guess I mean more avant-garde, less populist kinds of imagery, actions that would be more in line with the formal art thinking of the day. Then you talk about the immediacy of being able to come up with an idea and use it quickly. We grew up with that kind of thinking: protest songs, Bob Dylan and his terrible voice and his guitar—the voice of Everyman. A devastating concept at the time.

Miller: There's a weird mirroring of folk and punk—both basically populist movements, both three-chord phenomena. Basically the idea that anyone could pick up a guitar and play "Blowing in the Wind"—and most of us have.

Burnham: And it wasn't so important to be a virtuoso.

Miller: The thing to think now is where is all this going?

Burnham: Right now the art community is having to respond to the NEA crisis with Congress. All over the country people are trying to figure out the best way to affect the situation.

Miller: One lesson we've learned in L.A. is that we are working too slowly.

Burnham: In the NEA crisis, too, we've learned that we didn't act fast enough; in some ways, experience with ACT UP has taught us to strike faster and stronger. Do you think that's a spirit that's going to spread through all these crisis communities?

Miller: Yes. At any given time certain things have led the way to a new social energy. Obviously the civil rights movement did, and Vietnam, the women's movement, and gay liberation all came from that reinterpretation of Gandhi's reinterpretation of Tolstoy and Tagore's philosophies. So it's reincarnated in an interesting way.

Burnham: You're talking about ages—civil rights, Vietnam. Can we come to a thesis that activism is speeding up because of AIDS activism now?

Miller: I think it's been the front line for the last two or three years. It helped refuel and prepare people for women's health clinic defense actions. Also I know in all these cities ACT UP and its troops have been crucial for those actions. For whatever reason, more and more middle-class people are well versed in activism—and not in a romantic way, not for this month or for one event, but as an ongoing daily practice, almost a meditation.

Burnham: But we're so overextended.

Miller: Yes. And it's not going to get easier. You don't finish it, you don't acquire wealth and retire, you just keep working. That idea is very strong in ACT UP, that it is a great privilege to continue to work when people are dying. What *is* it when the ultimate reality is present—death? The great luxury of exhaustion, being able to work till you're tired is a great gift of life, because it means you get to go to sleep and wake up again and work some more. And think if any of us were being dragged kicking to an untimely death, how you would long for hard work and fatigue and hammers and typewriters and computers and the privilege and great joy of work. That keeps people from burning out. Because the ultimate burnout is when your friends die. You see very little burnout in AIDS activism—you do not have the luxury of burnout because the stakes are too high. This is true of all the communities in crisis, especially if you don't have a choice. I will not be offered a choice, my friends will keep dying. Hopefully I will not die because it's more fun to be doing this!

The other interesting thing is that every extra year I'm getting is like frosting; I definitely could have been dead two or three years ago.

Burnham: You must have been paralyzed with fear.

Miller: I was really scared in '84–'85. Then I started to come out of it. Leaving New York helped. There wasn't the feeling of what was to be done.

Burnham: What if we suddenly found an AIDS cure, would all of this activist spirit stop?

Miller: AIDS won't go away. There probably won't be a complete cure, there will be tiny increments of improvement, it seems. The crisis situation is going to stay. It seems like it's not going to be exponential—two years ago we thought conceivably by right now that 200,000 people would have died instead of 60,000—but they think a million people or so are HIV positive and some undetermined number of people will die. People are still getting sick. It's going to stay with us.

Burnham: What is the most important thing for us to do?

Miller: We have to be building on all the positive things we've been talking about—a continued vigilance, and the willingness to go to meetings when we don't want to. I don't have to fool myself to feel we're doing something worthwhile here at Highways. The bulk of our energy should be going into this project. We're doing something really interesting that's not bullshit. It's going to provide us with the tools to do anything else that's useful.

Burnham: What about your own work? What will be your emphasis?

Miller: Artists like me can't think that they're just working citizens who also happen to be making art. We have to keep refining the dialogue about what it means to be doing your own work but also contributing significant parts of your art energy to other activities, to keep refining that idea and do more within your communities. For me it's to keep on being one of many weird poet laureates of gay male sensibility in Southern California in the late twentieth century, which is more role than any artist should have to think they have to take on. You don't have to create the uncreated consciousness of your race. You have to be a little bit helpful in articulating a small corner of your time and community. And figure out what it is to parcel out your energy to your many activities and keep them all energized and alive. Say I got some fabulous career opportunity like an HBO special where they want to do the trilogy of my solos as a "masterpiece of late-twentieth-century performance art around gay themes" or something [laughs]—it would be a tragedy and a betrayal for me to leave other things I'm doing. It would be an equal tragedy for me to become only an administrator or a bureaucrat or an activist and not keep the work going. So those have to play off each other. That's a very useful two angels on your shoulder.

Linda Frye Burnham was the founder of High Performance
Magazine *and its editor until 1986. She is also a performance artist
and a widely published poet and writer, and a contributing editor
to* The Drama Review. *In 1989, she and Tim Miller founded
Highways Performance Space, located in the
18th Street Arts Complex.*

5

Jimmie Durham

Interviewed by Susan Canning

Born in Oklahoma in 1940, Jimmie Durham is a Native American sculptor, performance artist, writer, and political activist. Utilizing the languages of archaeology, ethnography, and history, disciplines that institutionalize the Indian, Durham's sculptures and performances comment upon the consumption of Native American culture. In his 1985 installation, On Loan from the Museum of the American Indian, *Durham parodied museum displays with his fabricated and found objects, packaged as "sociofacts" and "sciencefacts," upending the comforting image of the Noble Savage. For Durham's 1989 exhibition, "The Bishop's Moose and the Pinkerton Men," shown at Exit Art in New York, the artist recycled found objects and his own carvings into an intercultural form that he terms "neo-primitive, neo-conceptual."* A Certain Lack of Coherence, *a collection of Durham's artistic and activist writings, was recently published. Durham has refused to be constrained by categories of "Native American art," by predetermined boundaries of artistic or intellectual endeavor, or by comforting definitions of the role of the artist, the native, or the citizen. He has for some years lived primarily outside the United States, and now is based in Belgium, where this 1990 interview was conducted.*

Susan Canning: I know from your background that you have been involved with the Native American church and the AIM (American Indian Movement) and have taken an activist role in these groups. At the same time you have been a producer of art. What do you think is the role of an artist as activist and the relationship between political activism and art?

Jimmie Durham: I am really very confused about it. What I think I think is this: there is a cultural construct for art works that is the power apparatus, the apparatus that performs culturally. It doesn't perform by decrees. We are all oppressed and repressed by cultural means primarily. So it seems a reasonable way to attack the machine. But I don't do art so that I can screw the system. I do art because I do art. Because somewhere in your life, usually when you are a little kid, you become an artist without knowing what that means. Then you have to figure out how to do it responsively.

Canning: So it's not really subversion that you are after?

Durham: It's subversion that I'm after, absolutely. But I don't do art to be subversive. I would want to be the same subversive person no matter what I did. If I was a carpenter, I would want to be just as subversive. And it seems to me that's a responsibility we all have because there is this big old thing that is oppressing us. Why would you not work against it?

Canning: You speak of it as a responsibility. But the traditional definition of responsibility is to do what you are supposed to do, not to be subversive.

Durham: Well, obviously I wasn't trained that way. My family taught me to be a militant. Because we are against the United States, the United States is against us. So that was my first level of knowledge of the world, to be against the United States. Then when I got older, I could put it in more sophisticated terms.

Canning: So your background is one of resistance from the very beginning. Do you necessarily have to be outside of it to oppose it, or can you be inside to see how the system works?

Durham: I think the more that I participate in the world, the better I know ways that I might be subversive. When I was a teenager, I was a Cherokee activist. I was a naive resister. I didn't know very well how to resist. I didn't know what to resist. Things were in overly simplified terms for me. As I get older and more experienced out in the world, I think how to be more subversive when things come up.

Canning: One of the tactics of the avant-garde is sabotage; do you find it necessary to have a guerrilla mentality?

Durham: I think it's necessary, but in the art world, we artists do one of two things. We get too wrapped up in the art world exclusively and everything centers around our lives as artists, or we take our art out onto the streets and don't deal with the art world, don't deal with ourselves as artists that way. Both of those seem too limited to me. One of the things I hate about art is that it is so exclusive. It keeps itself very tight. Art has to refer to art to get seen. One way or another, that's what we always have. So any art that makes it is art that refers to other art. It's a closed system. It's a closed system maybe even more now that it pretends not to be a closed system. I think that it's more closed in a certain way.

Canning: Addressing the relationship between culture, nationality, colonialism, and power, you have written, "There is no Western culture but a power structure that pretends to be Western culture." What do you mean by this?

Durham: We tend to think that European culture is something that is there, but especially in the colonies, like the United States, Canada, all of Latin America, what we call modern culture, the dominant culture, we pretend has some organic roots in Europe, that it comes organically from European culture, that there is something bad about Europeans that made this dominant culture dominant. But it's not true, I don't think. I've lived in Europe and the people in the Alps, for example, are not part of that culture and that culture does not come from their culture. It really is an apparatus. It really is a machine. It does not evolve from some people and it does not belong to some people. It is not the "culture of the American people," it's just not there. It's something that is put onto people and everybody is alienated from it, everybody has to figure out how to struggle against it. Or you slash your wrists, or you become super alienated...

Canning: Or you make art?

Durham: Or you make art.

Canning: The critic Maureen Sherlock speaks of the machine of late modern capitalism and how it uses certain strategies, for example the language of capitalism, and how such a strategy has become so naturalized in our way of acting and being that it becomes a way of thinking. The point she makes is that everyone plays into it, whether they know it or not. Everyone still wants to participate, even though they are raging against it. That seems to be a dichotomy of some sort.

Durham: I think it's a necessary dichotomy. I think we have to agree to be confused about it. Because that system does control the world. It is the world. We can't afford to exclude ourselves from it. We have to be part of that world to be effective and because it's the world. I don't want to retire in any sense. I moved to Cuernavaca because I couldn't afford to live in New York. But I am not hiding in Cuernavaca. I write for publications in London and New York and I am very active in Mexico. I would feel the same way if I lived in New York. I would want to deal with Mexico, I would want to have a discourse with whatever is out there, everything that is out there.

Canning: This brings me then to the issue of language. Your most recent work, and your writing as well, deals a lot with the issue of language. First, do you have to know the language to subvert it? You have said before that you speak the language (English) well.

Durham: I'm very proud of that. For years and years I read the dictionary every morning with breakfast, so I know English very well. It's something that I learned on purpose and I'm proud of it.

Canning: Were you raised in the Cherokee language?

Durham: Cherokee and English, but Cherokee was the language that we used for ourselves. I didn't go to school much, so I didn't get terribly indoctrinated into what English was. We were able to resist that.

Canning: One of the things about studying another language is that when you perceive it as a system and you understand how it works, it leads you to understand how the people who use that language think.

Durham: I think that's absolutely true. What's always impressed me about American English is how manipulative it is. It has a way of pretending communication when most of the time it's manipulation and not communication, to get people to do something, to get people to buy something, to get people to believe something.

Canning: Do you think it is to get people to believe something or to think that they believe something?

Durham: Yeah, that's it. To hope that they'll believe it so they'll buy it. In fact, to make sure that they don't really believe it so that they are still alienated. People, white folks, used to come and ask us about our place, because we lived in the woods. We knew the woods because we were from the woods. And they wanted to know the names of things. A lot of times we didn't really know the names of things, but no matter what, all you could tell them about a particular tree or flower, its species, its habits, everything, couldn't satisfy them. They wanted the name of it, and if you could tell them any name, they were satisfied. No matter if you told them these are its habits, it was the name they wanted. It was a pretend knowledge that you would know something by calling it a fir tree. Of course, in what sense is it a fir tree? Where's the firness of the tree? If you know about a fir tree then you know it. The fact that it has an English name, with a long history, that's kind of esoteric knowledge that you don't really need unless you are studying word origins. Then you're studying the word, not the tree.

Canning: You wrote: "Understanding is the consumer product of your society. Once you've bought some understanding it's only natural to turn around and make a profit from it, psychological, economic or both." My question is: is it really understanding or is it confusion?

Durham: There is a way that we are taught to use knowledge. People say: "Knowledge is power." What a crazy concept. It's a dumb concept, actually. What are you talking about with "power"? Why is that word used? Why don't we use something more complex, another word. Why do we have to have this slogan?

Canning: Going back to the idea of language, you know that language is a tool to get there, so how can you negotiate within that system without doing the same thing yourself?

Durham: I don't think there is a constant answer and I don't think there is a clear answer. I am really confused. It's the time to be confused, but not in an inactive way: to see there are great complexities and to investigate more, to investigate more constantly, to not be satisfied with some little piece of something that makes you feel like you are powerful, that you've got the answer so you can move ahead. That's very dangerous.

Canning: In a sense, confusion has been marginalized in our society. Insanity or psychotic behavior is seen as being not rational, simply because rational is the way. It seems to me that confusion may be the subversive way of doing it.

Durham: I think so and for me it's a necessary subversion, because, when you start not knowing how you bought something, or how you were influenced by their crap, that's a dangerous situation because then you are moving without knowing a part of yourself that's doing the moving. A piece of you is acting that you don't even know about and these are dangerous times to act that way. So it seems that if one sees a responsibility with helping to subvert, then you have to constantly do a kind of self-analysis. How am I infected today? How do I get rid of that infection?

Canning: You speak of the "primitive" as a code or convention for interpretation. Do you want to talk about how you relate that to your work?

Durham: I think there is a European premise of the primitive which is different from the colonial, say, for example, Australia or the United States, these are colonial powers to me. Europe has a primitivism that it got by being conquered by Rome. But the colonies got their idea of "primitivism" because they carried out that ideal. Then they took over someone's land and killed those people in the process and pretended that they were not doing it. Which is a funny kind of set-up for a human being to deal with. So they were the psychopaths. The Europeans that came here were nuts, how could they not be? They were conquered by Rome and then they were conquered by the Church, they were tortured and burned for 1500 years. Every time they raised their hands to do something different, they got their guts cut out. They got it in school, they got beat up with a stick. Of course, you're going to be crazy after two thousand years of that. So then you come and take someone else's land, kill them, set up shop, and pretend that you didn't do it. So America has an idea of the primitive that's an absolutely operative idea, that actually drives the United States, and its idea has to be that it owns not only the primitives but primitivism. The United States has to see itself as the only expert on the savages because it must own the savages. Because it has to legitimatize its existence. Not once but continuously, it has to legitimatize its existence, because it continues to be a colonial set-up. But it can't admit it, because it would spoil the whole thing. That's why Native Americans are invisible. We are not invisible because we are a tiny minority. That's why our history is invisible, because the United States has to continually defend its existence and in that process it has to have consumed us. We have to be its heritage in a very serious intellectual and operative way.

I think the European concept of the primitive that this comes from is still operative and I think it's very close to the premise "women" and "artist"—different people who if they are allowed into the discourse would seriously fuck up the discourse. You have to subvert those people and their activities in order to keep the discourse rolling in the direction that it's supposed to be rolling. We don't think of artists that way. We don't think of the premise "artist" as being deliberately kept out of the discourse by the machinery. Yet it is very much and in similar ways as to "Indian" and "women" as premises. There you have a pedestal that you are put upon and admired and the pedestal is to keep you away from real life. And you are not really admired. Really you are hated, feared, abused. But you're given these little silly rewards as compensation that you're supposed to be satisfied with and they keep pushing. Like for example in the '50s where they pushed housewifery and how nice it was for ladies to sit around the coffee table, drinking coffee, being silly non-persons outside of the society. And they really sold this, locking that in. But that's what happens with art too. An artist is taught continuously that art really doesn't have any function in society, that art is very mysterious and then the rewards that you are offered are fame and fortune. Those are not legitimate rewards as or for human society. Your reward has got to be that you can function within society. That's the reward. If you as a woman are set up as a housewife with all the nice housewife things but then you can't function in the world, then what the hell kind of reward is that? Indians are the same way. People pretend to love us and they put us up on the pedestal of noble savage. The whole purpose is to exclude us because the discourse has to exclude us because we're going to say, "You're not legitimate" to the machine. That would be our intervention, that *is* our intervention—"You're not real, you're not legitimate," whereas the United States always has to say, "We are the most real, we are the most legitimate."

Canning: I was thinking, while you were talking, of commercials...that commercials train people to desire those nice things but at the same time they take away your identity while locking you into it, because then you are in debt.

Durham: And psychologically insecure, because you've got to have the next thing to keep functioning well, otherwise you can't in this society. If you watch the commercials about the right underarm deodorant, you might laugh at it, but then you start getting insecure. You might need that underarm deodorant... that's my problem, out there...not enough underarm deodorant.

Canning: But it seems that what you're involved with is an inversion of that. In the sense of using the language to invert it, to reveal the codes of the sexual, racial dispossession.

Durham: I try to do that, but in general it's a losing battle for me. Maybe I don't really expect to win any battles. Maybe I expect to win a few points here and there, to contribute my little piece to a bigger thing, but it's very hard because the system is so closed. Every time I do a show in New York, I get the most asinine things said...Indians don't do what I just did, or Indians shouldn't do what I just did. I did really ironic things, like "On Loan from the Museum of the American Indian," I mean crazy obvious things. Quite a few people thought it was on loan from the Museum of the American Indian and they were not dumb people.

Canning: About this idea of "On Loan" and how people thought that it was real, your work addresses the whole ethnographical and anthropological aspect of the "Indian." Don't people realize it's a parody?

Durham: Often people don't because we are taught not to be very subtle and parody takes a kind of subtle understanding. As well, people don't expect it from us, the Indians. People expect "the Noble Savage" in one way or another. They expect it and they want it. They don't want us to act bad. They want us to really reflect the stereotype. The same thing happens with performances that I've done. People reacted to them straightforwardly. It's because, as an Indian, people need for me to fit their stereotype. And the stereotype is that we are Noble Savages in the sense that we are very straightforward, very stoic, that we love America, that we are simpleminded, and that we are very spiritual, which, in real language, means that we are not sophisticated. We're kind of an animal that speaks only in a certain way that this kind of animal would speak. We're not supposed to be able to say normal things, or unusual things. We only say what we say in movies or books, the culture of the stereotype. We say stereotypical things.

Canning: You talk in your writings of history as a series of discontinuous facts and the significance is in the ordering.

Durham: I have come to think of history as a dysfunctional idea. There cannot possibly be history. What would we know of history as we think of history? As history is knowing what happened in the past, that's what we think history is. How could we possibly know what happened in the past? My mother just died, and I was with my three sisters and we were talking about our childhood and the things that we remembered in the past.

It was as though we were from different families. We grew up in the same house. We supposedly went through the same historical periods, but we didn't. And if each of us wrote the history of those years in that house, it would be different, really, really, different. What the hell do we mean by history? It's a new concept. One of the things that anthropologists have always been getting on our case about is that we didn't have a sense of history before the colonizers came to civilize us and I think that's true. It's pretty dumb to have an idea of history. We have to think more complexly than to think that we can know the past, because we can't. We believe whatever our situation causes us to believe and it may or may not be true. It may or may not be *the* really important things that happened. At the same time, because there is such an authoritative version of history, it's great fun to pull out other things that are hidden and left out and find a way to put them forward without making a countersign to their sign, because their signs are there. And I can't very effectively put up a countersign, I can't continually add footnotes to historical process because it is there, it is authorized history, and not much is going to change that.

Canning: Isn't it really a question of strategies?

Durham: Absolutely. I think one of the dangers of being artists at any time, we are taught that as artists, we create. That's a really dumb idea. Notions of creativity ought to be thrown out. I was raised differently, I come from a different culture. I'm an outsider who sneaks in, who continues to sneak in. I can't see that it's helpful. It's not possible for me to sit in my studio and make some art. Of course I can do that, I have skills, I can make things all day long. Then to just make things in my studio and not put them out in the world is an asinine idea. You're asking the world to speak your language and the world doesn't speak your language. It's just as if I insisted we conduct this interview in Cherokee. What would that do?

Canning: It would be a very one-sided conversation.

Durham: Exactly right. So I think it only makes sense that an artist makes his or her art in society, not in a studio. That makes it strategic all of the time. It always has to be strategic.

And to me what's mysterious is that we don't think that. We still think of ourselves as *the* creative people. We make our things and then we force them on the world and if they are great things the world will then appreciate them. That's an infantile idea that we've been given as the role that the artist plays. But if you say, "Here I am an artist, I am an artist in society, whether I would like to be or not," then you have to think of your work as being ways to investigate real situations. Ways that deal with objects and visual things primarily, not with text primarily and not with textual investigations primarily. Then I have to figure out what sort of things to investigate and how to investigate them. That demands a constant attempt at discourse with society. If I go back home and make something and then give it to the world and say here it is, I can't see why I would do that, I can't see what I would get from it, except I could sell it and get a little piece of money...

In the '70s, when there first became this fad called political art, this little category called political art hid the idea that everything else was political art also. The category said that political art was a painting or a sculpture that had a slogan on it, that's what political art came to be defined as and everything else was not political art. Artists are taught to be stupid and we have to recognize that. Just like the housewife in the '50s was taught to be stupid. We have to try to stop being stupid because it is not interesting to be stupid.

Canning: Turning to the discourse of modernism...On one level you are talking about what it is to be an artist, the tools, the language. But then there is also modernism and the discourse of the modern artist. Do you see your work as an inversion of that, in a "postmodern" sense?

Durham: I don't like modernism. I don't like what it's done. It's been a very oppressive agenda. But I don't think it should be finished with. I totally distrust the people who are celebrating its death and at the same time celebrating a new style which is recognizably postmodern. If we say that modernism is an agenda, postmodernism has to be a situation, not an agenda. So the situation has to include everything that the agenda did not include. The agenda goes away, therefore everything is there.

That's what the New York art world is saying that it does but it doesn't do that. There are postmodernist styles and there are enforced postmodernist styles, that's just modernism, that's just continuing the agenda. However, modernism can be very useful as a cultural tool for moving into the world in a better way. I think that Kay Walkingstick is a good example of that. I think her work is very valuable, because she's a very good modernist painter. And we as Indians need that. We need that as a way to free up things, in a way that my work doesn't necessarily do for us. And certainly the different Indian art schools that have developed in the last twenty years all lock you into a stereotype of modern art, of a way of being. They are very informative, these Indian styles. They inform people how to be Indian and that's very dangerous.

Canning: Another issue you deal with is authenticity...

Durham: It's a funny search, this search for authenticity. It's very funny in the United States with us. Part of the United States myth about us is that we are not authentic. Historically, Indians of the past are considered to be the only authentic Indians, but at the same time, they're not very authentic because they did not really exist. The myth says that the United States came to the wilderness, without any Indians in it. At the same time it says that the only real Indians are those they didn't see there. It's really a convoluted bit of craziness. But people need us to act authentically. People need to search for authentic things. Us primitives are the holders of these authentic things, this authenticity. Except of course we're not. It's a search that goes on and on for the authentic this, for the authentic that. It's another silly thing. What could they possibly be talking about? an artifact? a way of being? I can't understand what is in people's minds when they are looking for this authenticity. But we're given it, we have it inflicted upon us. So Indians want to be authentic, to see ourselves as authentic, especially for those who see us as authentic. It's very dirty, it's very destructive. So I want to subvert whenever I can think of ways that I might, the whole concept of authenticity, at the same time to try to call attention to how silly they're being.

Canning: Humor plays a major role in your work—it is ironic, sarcastic, subversive, and healing. Could you comment on that?

Durham: I think it can be but I also think you have to be careful with it. I have to be careful with it. Cherokees are very funny people, we're always using humor. It's really part of us. I think it's always been there. We're always making puns in Cherokee. We're always playing with the language. I think it also comes as a defense from what we've been through the last three hundred years. Like the Jewish people it's a survival tactic and that's where it gets dangerous. Because we can defend too much. So I'm always wondering if I've overdone it in a show. And sometimes I'm using humor very consciously and sometimes I'm not. Sometimes it just happens as a cultural thing. If it gets to be where things are too funny, where humor is too much constantly there, then it can lose its bite, it can lose its power as a survival tactic, lose any point to it. I think there is a way to use humor. I think it can be more subversive than a lot of other things.

Susan Canning *is an arts writer living in New York.*

6

Carrie Mae Weems

Interviewed by Susan Canning

As an artist who utilizes photographic media to visualize her ideas, Carrie Mae Weems often presents her work in conceptual exhibitions whose formal context creates an environment for her thematic concerns. Family Pictures and Stories *(1978–1984) consists of numerous photographs of the artist's extended family, arranged like snapshots in a walk-in photo album, accompanied by her reminiscences and retelling of family tales. In* Ain't Jokin *(1988–1990), Weems illustrates racist jokes with a literal directness that confronts the viewer with offhanded bigotry while simultaneously implicating him/her within the social praxis of such activity. Turning from the manner in which racial intolerance is manifested and passed along via language and cliché, in* Colored People *(1990) Weems explores the dual nature of caste and color within the African-American community. For* And 22 Million Very Tired and Very Angry People *(1991), first exhibited at The New Museum of Contemporary Art, Weems fills a whole room with large format Polaroid prints and red banners, each with a different text. The result, which physically compels the viewer to look not only at the images but also up at the banners, allows for a multitude of readings and voices. In* Untitled *(1990), shown at P.P.O.W. and at the 1991 Whitney Biennial, Weems creates a fictitious photo-narrative whose often humorous but emotionally intense story of a romantic relationship reflects the artist's concern for visualizing the lives of African-American women. Her work has continued to have a unique power to embody difficult social truths and deep personal experiences, creating resonances that have broad significance in an era for which the idea of "community" is often used to mask reactionary agendas. The following conversation took place in 1993.*

Susan Canning: One of the things that I find interesting in your work is the use of space. *Family Stories*, for example, is almost like entering into your family photo album. *And 22 Million Very Tired and Very Angry People* is a complete installation. In other pieces, space is formed through the construction of a narrative between the various photos, creating a space almost like an envelope, or bookends.

Carrie Mae Weems: I think there is a psychological space created for myself and the viewer. It's a psychological space that works when you've found its rhythm. That's the thing that allows you to move through it and to feel wrapped up in it. It's like listening to music. Trinh Minh-ha says in "Living in the Round" that everything about the space where people live their lives had to do with the rhythm of the space. You know when people were working on chain gangs, there was a lead singer and a pulse beat was constantly going that established a psychological space for you to enter so that you could almost forget about what you were doing. I am interested in that thing, whatever that "thing" is. Sometimes it works and sometimes it doesn't. But I think that there can be, whether it happens in my work often enough is questionable, but there can be a real solidity and a wonderful sound, a visceral sound, that takes place between how the text reads as a piece, whether on a wall or hanging from a banner, and how it crosses the room to meet up with another photograph. I think that I am very much interested in that, probably all artists are, in sort of surrounding the viewer and yourself in a world to deal with very particular ideas and notions. You have to be into the mess of the thing.

Canning: What about the authority of your voice—that it's female, that it's African-American, that it deals with issues of class, that it's vernacular?

Weems: I think it's simply my way of sounding out and allowing a certain resonance to take place that wouldn't otherwise. I don't think about it from an "I" position, I feel it's a communal voice, a voice of a group, a voice of a class, and that I know what that voice sounds like because I've come from that group, that class. I know what that language is. I suppose I'm usually thinking of it as that collectivity.

Canning: And the collective voice is female, African-American...

Weems: Well, it is and it isn't. There is often a male's voice that intervenes, that has to be there. It makes sense because then you have to deal with the mess of things. There could be a clearly defined, delineated female voice, and then there's a sort of male voice. For instance, the male voice in *Untitled* is really wonderful. Without his voice in the shit, it wouldn't fly, it wouldn't go anywhere. There's definitely something that she's on to, but he has a say in her shit, too, about how it's going to fall. And *her* position is to move back and to give him room to speak. And in *22 Million* it is a conglomerate of voices, all kinds of voices, coming from all over the place, and it's not always a black voice. That's probably the one I feel most comfortable with. I love the idea of penetrating the "king's English," but that's not the only thing. I think people would prefer to think about it as being the only thing because then it contains me, in what I call "nigger space," but I really don't want to stay there because that's not all of who I am.

The things that interest me and the things I try to play around with have to do with the quality of certain kinds of voices from certain kinds of places. Probably more often than not, it's a female voice but it's not always a female voice and it's not always a black voice. I guess that notion of the multiplicity of sound in a voice is crucial and that's probably one of the most important things to me politically and socially.

Canning: But nevertheless, the voices that you activate aren't authorized, aren't given their due.

Weems: It's like penetrating the "king's English." The reality is that we are living in a democracy where most of us are supposed to be silent. That's what democracy is, right? So that anything that intervenes in that is a certain kind of amateur authority. But the thing that is remarkable is that we all claim space, all peoples attempt to claim space. Whether you do it through rap, etc., how you speak is the important thing. The issues of activating voices, or giving them authority, I really don't care about that so much as intervening, just intervening in a certain kind of way, wanting to say a certain kind of something, and hoping it may get heard. Probably ninety-nine percent of the time it doesn't, but sometimes it does get heard. Sometimes it falls just on the right drums at the right moment so that something might happen, something may pull you, the audience, me even, to initiate some kind of action based on the quality of that sound. It's like listening to Martin Luther King speak and then going out and organizing a bus strike or something. Things can get done.

Canning: So you see yourself as a catalyst and your work as being a catalyst?

Weems: It has the possibility of being that, under the right circumstances. It certainly gives you pause. There's some stuff you have to deal with when coming to the work, and then once you leave there are some things you have to think about and then you go home and talk to your husband, or your kids, your boyfriend. It does something, it's not just on the wall.

Canning: Where do you interject your own language?

Weems: The collective and the I are both in there. You can't talk about something unless you've experienced it on some psychological or physical level. So that's where I think I come in, as a certain conduit for a kind of experience, because I'm a real working-class girl, a "cotton-pickin, corn-pickin negro," you know. I know what that experience is, it's not abstracted from some Marxian text.

Canning: I see a change in the location of the voice, from the narrator in *Family Pictures* to a more declarative voice in *Ain't Jokin*, to a cataloguer in *Colored People*, to an orator or dissident in *And 22 Million Very Tired and Very Angry People*. Do you think this is true?

Weems: Yeah, because in each piece, voice and text has a very particular role to play. In *Ain't Jokin* I'm really just pulling from Anglo-American folklore, as opposed to *Family Pictures and Stories* where I am pulling from my mother's memory, as opposed to *22 Million* which pulls from history and direct quotation, not folklore. Each piece demands a very particular kind of voice. My family's stories would be completely inappropriate in *22 Million*. It just wouldn't make any sense, that quality of sound wouldn't make any sense. I think in that piece it was really important to rely on the viewer's and the reader's sense of pacing. When you read it you have a certain sound too, a certain voice. It creates its own space in some ways for each individual.

Canning: What about the way the text positions the viewer to read and see. I assume that you purposefully implicate the viewer. How did you get to that point?

Weems: I think it happened fairly early on, in trying to deal with the issue of spectatorship, in where are people placed, in trying to bring them into it. If you decide that we are all party to the crime then it makes sense that we all are held accountable. You could then point to the viewer and say "you" and "us" as opposed to "they." The thing that troubles me more about the advent of postmodernism is that there is always a "they," "them over there" sensibility, but it's never about us and how we fucked up, how we allowed a certain amount of victimization to take place to begin with.

Canning: It's not only implicating the viewer but also activating the viewer.

Weems: You have to move around a bit. You have to do something.

Canning: So it's not passive. Do you see that as part of the politics of it?

Weems: I'm not sure if I've really thought of it in that way. I like the idea of the viewer being active. I'm a political artist, that's what I do. There's a part of making that's quite wonderful. The aesthetic experience is a wonderful experience, but that's certainly not enough. But it's what viewers come away with, what they learn, what they understand, that they begin to question, that matters most to me about being involved in the whole thing. It goes back to your earlier question, about the work being a catalyst. Well it's hopefully a catalyst to memory, a catalyst to some sort of action, a part of a force, a movement for something bigger. It's only a drop in the bucket, relatively speaking, but I think it grants a sense of unity since each of us can contribute our small part that will make up the total, right? That can effect change, then that becomes our moral obligation. You strike where you can. Hopefully it's just enough to rock the boat, just enough to ask some real fundamental questions.

And maybe it isn't. Maybe I'm fooling myself, but I'm really hoping that it asks the questions that need to be asked. Not that the work needs to ask, but that we as social beings trying to figure out how to live on this god-damned planet need to ask about how we go about doing it.

Canning: And you do that through actively implicating the viewer. For example *Ain't Jokin* are photographs of very literal images and really awful racial epithets or jokes, so that there is no way that you don't get it.

Weems: Because that becomes the shit, that really becomes the shit. You know there have been more mamas than we can shake a stick at that look at their kid and say, "you ain't never going to be shit," and there is everything you've ever thought of when you see a black person with a watermelon or a chicken. You know we all occupy a position relative to the stereotype. That's what I think is interesting about that piece.

I think it's probably the best piece I've ever done. It's so unmediated. It's just so naked. That's the thing that upsets people more than anything. It exposes the wounds so deeply. I think that's one reason that people react to it the way that they do, and one reason they try to ban it as much as they possibly can. On the other hand, people try to show it as much as they can. There's a real issue about that work. It's very uncomfortable, but then dealing with our real shit is always uncomfortable. But I think that idea of occupying a number of different sites, that there are a number of different sites to be occupied around a given body of work is a very interesting idea.

I suppose that the same thing is true though no matter what the work. I mean, a black family experiencing *Family Pictures and Stories* has a different thing to say to me than a white person experiencing the work. And certain black people find it really offensive, depending on where they are coming from. So this idea that you try to hum a collective voice is an important idea, but yet you always have to get more specific— "well whose collective voice are you talking about?" "What voice are you talking about specifically, dahlin," since each of us does occupy many different sites, locations, positions. I suppose this is what I've been thinking about more and more. I think that the movement has to be toward a united front, so that you form collectives upon what is agreed upon. It's a limited partnership, but it's there.

Canning: What was the reaction to *Colored People*? My own reaction was that it had that double take, because on the one hand it was dealing with issues of caste, of power and hierarchy, but at the same time they are incredibly beautiful in color and tone. And the naming of color, from a white person's point of view, is all about the beauty of the color. So there is a double message, a double language, a double thing, because it is also a way of selecting, of saying one is better than, or one is less than. Yet at the same time, it is part of the culture—how people name you or describe you. But in a certain way you are also implicating this selection as creating the system.

Weems: It doesn't create the system, it expresses the system. That's very different. And then it takes the system out. So you can start out with "High Yellow" and "Magenta." It becomes the way caste is in place but is also completely ridiculous and wonderful. That it sort of folds in on itself, that it critiques its own language, and its own position. It's just like this little drop of color. It doesn't matter which one you are. They're all crazy, they're all wonderful, they're all different. I get every kind of reaction. People are interested in them. I mean they are all beautiful, they're all children. There's nobody in there over eighteen. That was one of the points, of dealing with the idea of color as it exists among young children, young people as they struggle to get their identity. There hasn't been any controversy. Nobody has written about them.

Canning: There is a certain irony in your work. What would you say is its role in your work?

Weems: To point up irony, that which is ridiculous, that which is nonsensical. To get to the wit and humor of it, because it's all of that which makes it understandable and approachable. I think it's the irony that makes it approachable.

Canning: How do you see humor as working in your art?

Weems: I think that the work is deadly serious, except that it uses humor to bring you into it. It's like telling a joke at a party, it breaks the ice. You tell a joke and they tell a joke and then a whole series of conversations can ensue from that place. Like they say, sometimes you can catch more flies with honey than with vinegar. I think that that's true. First of all, I love humor, just because I think it's great, but also, as in folklore, it becomes a way to deal with very difficult issues that we wouldn't ordinarily feel comfortable broaching or dealing with. So it provides us with a kind of arena once again to discuss the undiscussible in a way that is socially sanctioned through humor, through irony, proverb, or any other folklore element. I think that's its importance, its beauty, and its wonder, that it allows us this very special space to interact.

Canning: That tension is what I found provocative. For example there is a certain absurdity in *Ain't Jokin* of that literal image of a woman with a chicken.

Weems: They're really hilarious. The humor is much more wicked because it has much more to do with the insidious nature of the devastatingly real effects of humor on a race of people. Because the jokes were not just used as a social barometer to talk about black folk, it's been used as a way of annihilating them and keeping them completely in check. So it's no wonder when they walk through Brooklyn to protest the death of Yusef Hawkins that they're waving watermelons and chickens at the people passing through.

Canning: But in the juncture between those two points you laugh and yet you catch yourself at the same time.

Weems: Yeah, well that's the nice part of it. Because hopefully what you realize is that you're laughing, but then what are you laughing at exactly? Why is this funny? Why is it not funny now, but it was funny last night when my girlfriend told me that joke? That's the shit. Because humor circulates in very interesting patterns.

Canning: Let's move to your concern for social issues and social change. I read that some of the issues you are interested in were revolution, African-American achievement, civil rights, and affirmative action. Would you say that those are the main issues of concern?

Weems: I'll just say, those and others. Let's keep it open, as concerns are always spiralling out. I think the idea is that if you can operate within your given sphere, as a catalyst, then there are possibilities—simply that, that there are possibilities. Because we all know essentially that something's got to give. Now what is it exactly? What one does then is to posit some possibilities about what it might be, where it might go, what might be some things we need to consider along the way. So I think that where maybe I am starting from is trying to understand the relative place of a new kind of democracy. I'm really interested in this idea of forging a very different kind of democracy that has as its base a very highly developed sense of what is possible on the planet with all of us living on it with different needs, desires, and aspirations. How do we take care of our own? How do we take care of our constituencies with other constituencies in mind that we might not completely agree with? It's slow in coming, but it's worthwhile. And that we are involved in the process of change. So to talk about the future is ridiculous, because the future is now. It is a part of now.

Susan Canning is a writer and art historian living in New York.

7

Carmen Lomas Garza

Interviewed by Jennifer Easton

Carmen Lomas Garza is a Chicana artist. Born in 1948 in Kingsville, Texas, she currently lives in San Francisco. Throughout her career, she has insisted on the importance of both social action and personal artistic achievement, and she has often spoken of the difficulty of balancing the need to work in the studio with the drive to improve education and other aspects of life for the children in her community. Her own work is not overtly political; she portrays daily life in Mexican-American communities in paintings that have a lively intimacy. She is an artist, though, who refuses to limit herself to the studio: her interventions in social and political life are achieved as an activist and organizer. Social and aesthetic missions are not always easy to reconcile. For example, Lomas Garza points to a paradoxical trend in sponsorship of the arts, in an era of dwindling pools of public money and badly strained resources among corporate and foundation arts funds: while there is currently greater recognition of the traditionally underfunded cultures and ethnicities, the support tends to be funneled toward art as social programming at the expense of direct support of artists to create their work. Lomas Garza addresses this problem as well as the broader issues of the socially committed artist, and she also offers concrete examples from the Hispanic community of the potential for artists acting individually and collectively to have a substantial impact on both cultural life and the broader social realm. Jennifer Easton interviewed Lomas Garza in 1994.

Jennifer Easton: You came of age as an artist during the height of the Chicano Movement in the late '60s to early '70s. Could you give some background on your community involvement, particularly as an artist?

Carmen Lomas Garza: I should start all the way back in 1969 when I was still an undergraduate student at Texas A&I University and the Chicano Movement was going very strong there. The Mexican American Youth Organization (MAYO) was very active. The MAYOs were similar to the Brown Berets in California. That year, there was the first national conference where different MAYOs from all over Texas and a few other states were invited to attend. The leader of the MAYOs wrote to one of my art faculty members about putting a show together of Chicano art. The faculty felt that a Chicano should do this, and so they gave me the letter and said, "Here, we think you should do this." I had never put a show together, I didn't know anything about curating, and I was able to put a show together of mostly Chicano students from the University. Many were not active as Chicano artists, but were interested in learning, and then some were very much aware and had been participating with the MAYOs. So I was able to put a show together and took it to the conference. The leader of the organization helped make some of the transportation arrangements. I hung the show, manned the show, slept in the room where the show was installed, guarded it, cleaned everything, and learned a tremendous amount. I met many MAYOs who to this day I continue to have very strong friendships with. So this was my first experience dealing with the community, dealing with the issues we were all trying to deal with, everything from the Vietnam War, to problems with the migra (Immigration and Naturalization Services), and big problems with the educational system.

Easton: Your artistic training was very Eurocentric, I imagine?

Lomas Garza: Yes. It was very classical and academic, very European-centered, just like everyone's curriculum for art education. It was ironic because we were so close to Mexico. It's still going on, things have not changed very much, and it is very depressing. We have screamed and yelled to get more, at least with the art departments. The anthropology departments have been dealing a lot more with the arts of the Americas, but in the art departments they are still very slow about presenting full semester required courses on the history of the arts of the Americas.

Easton: So continuing with your community involvement, what next?

Lomas Garza: Soon after the conference, as a result of the conference, a committee was established to develop an alternative college, Colegio Jacinto Trevi, in South Texas. So I dropped out of school and went to that college and started taking classes while at the same time I was teaching the MAYOs silkscreening, drawing, and printmaking. All these MAYOs were mostly high school drop-outs and push-outs, some junior high and some college level. That took a lot of energy because I had never taught before, and everything was new, the whole situation was new. It was very tense because the whole Colegio was under a lot of scrutiny, including by police.

Easton: How long was the college active?

Lomas Garza: The college was active several years. I was there about nine months, then decided to come back to the University to try and finish my degree. There was a spin-off group from that original Colegio that formed another college, Juarez-Lincoln Center in Austin, that I became involved with. There I was doing mostly graphic design and putting shows together that were exhibited there. It was lower key. Then I taught in the public schools for a while, went to graduate school in Washington state, and ended up here at the Galería de la Raza. That is where I spent the most time, from 1976 to 1981, at the Galería Community Art Gallery. I was a volunteer for about four months, as long as my money could last, and then they hired me part-time, although I was actually working full-time. I helped with every aspect of the organization from helping to write proposals, to painting walls, cleaning toilets, selling in the store, talking with artists, and curating exhibitions. Another Chicana, Maria Piñero, started there at the same time. We brought in the feminist element. We opened it up to more exhibitions by Chicana artists, did large group exhibitions.

I also curated the first Frida Kahlo exhibition in 1978. Of course I didn't do it alone; the staff helped with all aspects of the show, and there was a committee to help with the curating. I spent a lot of time helping other Chicano and Latino artists exhibit their work, and some young neighborhood artists, kids who were trying to get into graffiti art. It was a fantastic learning experience, but it was also very draining. I still continued to do my artwork, and fortunately I managed to get some artist-in-residence grants from the California Arts Council sponsored by the Galería de la Raza, and also by RAP (Real Alternatives Program), an alternative high school in San Francisco where I taught for a year. A lot of the kids who were students there were push-outs and drop-outs, a lot of emotional and drug problems.

Easton: So you were doing an artist-in-residence, but at the same time you were working as a teacher/mentor, still doing the community outreach.

Lomas Garza: Yeah. So I still kept on trying to do my work. Finally in 1987, I had my last artist-in-residence grant and I decided not to try for any more. I had five years of them on and off, and that was a tremendous help, because while teaching in the different organizations I could continue to do my artwork. In 1987 I decided to do it solo, just depend on my artwork, exhibit, try to get grants, fellowships, that sort of thing, try to make sales and lecture at conferences—a lot of going to conferences dealing with the Movement—lecture at public schools with a lot of Mexican-American kids, and lecture at universities also. I continue to be involved. Recently the Galería de la Raza started a program called "Regeneration," and they're trying to do a lot of direct mentoring with young Chicano/Latino artists here in the Bay Area. Students from the San Francisco Art Institute, UC-Berkeley, Stanford, San Francisco State University, and former students.

Easton: Sounds like you're still trying to fill in the gaps of the university systems.

Lomas Garza: Exactly, doing a lot of mentoring where we're trying to provide an alternative, discussions about what has happened with the Chicano Movement, what has been happening and what continues to happen in the institutions of art. We did it because of the students. A core group of students who had been interns to some of us were very frustrated at the Art Institute and wanted to get more direct input from *veteranos* of the Movement. We realized that these students represented many more that had the same problems. So with the help of this core group of students who took on the responsibility of doing most of the organizing and recruiting, we have been doing meetings and workshops. Judy Baca came from Los Angeles, I did a workshop for them on the business of art. That's another issue that's not being covered.

Easton: You have said that you felt in the '80s there was a lull in young Chicano artists coming up. Do you ascribe this to the political or economic climate?

Lomas Garza: I'm not sure how to explain it. I think as we get further from the '80s, we can start to analyze what happened. But now there is a surge of young Chicanos who are definitely interested, and who are much better read—this core group I was talking about, very aware, very much interested, very aggressive in finding out what happened and wanting to get information from the *veteranos*. At Stanford there's a conference next weekend, "Chicanos and Activism," where we will be talking about what we have done over the years as far as activism in the community. If you look at all the centros and the Galería and The Mexican Museum (San Francisco), all of these institutions were started by artists, and a lot of them are still there. But a lot of them have "burned out," and some have been pushed out; some organizations got so big that they needed more expertise than the artists could provide. So there have been some bitter partings, but I think in some cases it was for the better. And in some cases it was sad that it had to happen that way, but the organizations have grown and they're so difficult to keep funded. There are a lot of Chicana and Chicano artists who have spent a lot of precious time doing this. We need it, but at the same time, we also feel an obligation to do it. It's very hard sometimes because you feel at times that you really want to concentrate more on your artwork than be on committees and go to meetings and do all this kind of work. What happened to me is when I decided to concentrate on my work, I just zoomed, I produced so much work and received so much more exposure because I was very aggressively pursuing this. It was very hard to say no to a lot of invitations to get involved with lectures and boards. In the long run I feel that I have reached many more people by concentrating on my artwork and doing the publications.

Easton: It seems when the funding dollars are short, direct support to artists to produce work is the first to disappear, with the focus left on the support of art as social programming. Would you agree that the cultivation of talent of the broad spectrum of artists from different ethnicities and cultures is as important, if not more so, to avoid the loss of sustained cultural artistic legacy?

Lomas Garza: Well for example, all of the paintings in the children's book *Family Pictures/Cuadros de Familia* (1990, with Harriet Rohmer) I did during the periods while supported by grants. I did some while I was an artist-in-residence for the California Arts Council (CAC), so I was teaching in the community, but I was also doing my artwork, and so it gave me a chance to build a body of work to a certain degree. Then when I stopped the artist-in-residence, I really moved on and got an NEA grant; that came at a very crucial time when I was starting to be on my own, it helped me get back up on a more even level so I could produce a lot. So the artwork from the children's book is from those two periods. So here I was being supported by the artist-in-residency grant from the CAC and the fellowship from the NEA, and now that book has reached thousands of kids. They have printed 40,000 copies and now it's in paperback and parts have been reprinted in textbooks. So an even greater number of children have seen the paintings. So the funding was very important. Now I'm at the point where I rely much more heavily on sales of my artwork; I spend a lot of time selling directly to collectors, and through a couple of galleries, but even with the galleries it's hard because they take fifty percent. So I keep real tight control on what I let go through the galleries. It's very time-consuming, but it's something that's necessary.

Easton: Now that you're more involved with it, do you think the gallery system runs counter to the goals of community and art?

Lomas Garza: There are a lot of pros and cons. I'm not a muralist, I don't work in large scale. What I do to reach the community is prints. Prints are something I have been doing since I was an undergraduate and realized the value of multiples; I could be involved with the Chicano movement and exhibit prints at many different locations—conferences, libraries, centros, and still be able to sell some of them. So I could reach a really wide audience.

Easton: I recently read an interview with Rebecca Rice by William Cleveland, "Rebecca Rice: Building Bridges" (*Art in Other Places*, Westport, Conn.: Praeger, 1992. 258ff.). She is an actress and activist, and one of the issues she addressed had to do with multicultural programming and its tendency to reinforce the notion of ethnic "sameness." In another of your interviews you addressed a similar issue. Could you go into that a bit?

Lomas Garza: Well, I've been doing this for twenty-five years, and the multicultural label is just a new label—the idea of trying to educate people about their culture and the different aspects of their culture. There are many different kinds of Chicano art, different artists have different answers to what it is. And there are different needs within the artists and within the community. There's nothing new. But you have to start somewhere and at least it's a beginning. Again we will have to fight against it becoming stagnant, against saying "this is the only way it is" when that's not true. There's a wide spectrum. For example, my artwork does not have overt political statements in it. It deals more with just the common, everyday life of a Mexican American. I felt twenty-five years ago that that aspect of Chicano art was being overlooked, that we needed to make not only the political statements about the injustices or the Vietnam War or the migra, but we also needed to make statements about the everyday life that we take so much for granted, that at times is very similar to other cultures and at times is very unique.

Easton: Yet often the work of artists of particular cultures is criticized for being too much about ethnic issues and not about "art," which is something I believe you have had direct experience with; and other times artists are told their work is not ethnic enough. These criticisms can be levelled from both inside and outside the culture. Is this something you are conscious of when doing your own work?

Lomas Garza: To me the most important thing that I have been doing as a Chicana artist is reaching the Mexican-American population. The greatest need is there. To me it's a bigger challenge to have a show at the museum in Corpus Christi, Texas than to show at the Whitney, because there I would reach the Mexican-American population that needs to see my work, that needs to get the reinforcement, the inspiration, that confirmation of who we are, more than in New York. All the criticism doesn't matter, it doesn't do anything to me because all I need to see is a Mexican-American family looking at my work and immediately start discussions with their kids, where the kids might not recognize it, or the kids do recognize it and they can turn back to their parents and say for example: "We did that last week, we had the *curandera* come to our house and she helped my mother." That's it, that's all I need. So when someone asks me how I feel about my success, meaning my recent ability to exhibit in museums and places like that that have been closed before, I say that's just a more recent form of success. I have been having successes since the beginning when I started to show my prints and Chicanos could see themselves in the prints and collect them. But there was this recognition that to them it was all they needed, the image was very much a part of their lives.

Easton: What has been the most effective way that you have seen of bringing the community and art together?

Lomas Garza: There are so many different ways you can get your image out to an audience, everything from the traditional form, which is a museum...actually, that's not that traditional. The most traditional form is through the art of the people, the folk art. That was one of the inspirations for the kind of work I do. My mother used to do the *loteria tablas* (playing cards), which was artwork framed under glass. You played on the artwork. They were images that dealt with the lives of the people who were playing on them. To me the artists who did those cards were reaching that circle of people. There are so many different ways...the museums, the art of the people; then the publications, the books, now there's TV and film. The children's book has reached quite a lot of kids, I can't begin to tell you. They would have never had a chance to see my traveling show or go to Galería de la Raza, but they have been able to see the artwork in the books. If we talk about the general population, the art of the people, there is the art in the churches, in the business establishments, restaurants, on and on.

Easton: Now that you have backed away from the day-to-day direct community arts involvement and are having to deal more with the art establishment, how are you finding that?

Lomas Garza: It's a whole other format, and I have always felt, and a lot of Chicano artists, though not all of us, have felt that the museums should have been open to the work we have been doing. It's only been recently, in the past five to seven years that the museums have been opening up, and a lot of that has to do with political pressure. Now there are more numbers to put the pressure on these institutions of art and it's starting to affect their pocketbooks. It's something we have been fighting for all along, the exhibiting of artists of color. Now they're opening up, some because they really believe in showing the work of artists of color and reaching out and bringing it into the museum, some only because it's hurting their pocketbooks—begrudgingly doing it, I can tell immediately the difference. You just have to listen for a while and ask questions and you get the gist of what they are truly feeling. It took me a while to learn to decipher that, so when a museum or an institution of art is sincerely interested, I work really hard to meet them halfway, at times even more than halfway. When the idea for my show was being discussed at Laguna Gloria Art Museum in Austin, Texas, and they approached the gallery where I show in Austin, Galería Sin Fronteras, about the idea of a show, I knew they were under a lot of pressure. They had not been showing that many Chicano or Mexican-American artists and they were right there in

Austin. They had shown a couple before me, and had done solo shows, but for the majority, they had not done anything special. So I put a couple of conditions on them. I was very honored to do the show, but at the same time I felt they were going to have to work very hard to make sure that the Chicano community of Austin was involved and benefited from this exhibition.

Easton: How do you feel that went?

Lomas Garza: Well I went nine months in advance to introduce the curator of the exhibition to some key Chicanos in Austin. I introduced them to each other, set up meetings so that we could discuss ideas for the exhibition, what we could do, what they could do to help the museum and what the museum could do for the different organizations.

Easton: So you were doing their outreach for them?

Lomas Garza: Here I was the artist taking time off, travelling from San Francisco, to introduce the curator to some key local people. People who were sitting back-to-back, I made them turn around and face each other and work together. A thousand people showed up at the opening. They had never had that kind of turnout for a solo show.

Easton: Have they continued the dialogue with the community?

Lomas Garza: To a certain degree yes. They have been trying to get some of those people to be on the board, trying to get more of the artists into the exhibitions. I have seen this again and again. The "Hispanic Art in the United States" exhibition at the Museum of Fine Arts in Houston opened up their eyes to the tremendous response from the Hispanic community. There was such a great need for some relevance at that museum for the Hispanic community that when the show came around, there was a tremendous response, and they were flabbergasted. I traveled around with the show because I was reinstalling the "Frida Kahlo Ofrenda," so I got to see how the museums interacted with the local Hispanic communities and how they interacted with us, the artists, who had to come in advance to do the installations. It was quite an eye-opener. With the museums there's another level of education. Not only am I dealing with the museum staff, but I am also dealing with the Chicanos and

Latinos in the corporate sector who are trying to fund exhibitions. Now there are more of my Chicano and Latino peers in the corporations who have some say-so as to where monies can be spent. But they're not artists, they're not in the arts field, they have their agendas and their needs, but at the same time they have a certain amount of responsibility to the Chicano/Latino community, la Raza. Again I have to spend time educating them, prompting them to give monies over to the projects I'm working on.

Easton: Seems like the challenge is harder now than what you undertook with the community.

Lomas Garza: It's difficult, but not as difficult as dealing with the community on a grassroots level. With the corporate people, they already know some of the game. It just takes a lot of talking to them and appealing only on particular levels. There's the level of "you're reaching a certain audience," and you're talking about economics and the buying power of that population. They understand that. It's just the fine-tuning you have to be careful about. For example, with the celebration of the quincentennial of Columbus, you had to tell these corporate people, "Look, there's a lot of brouhaha going on, but you have to look at what really happened, the history of what happened as a result of the colonization and how that has affected our communities for the past 500 years. You have to be careful about putting Columbus on a pedestal."

Easton: It seemed, at least here in Los Angeles, that the focus was on the problematic issues of colonization and the legacy of Columbus. It was more of a year that celebrated indigenous populations.

Lomas Garza: And it was great that it happened, the timing was right. People were ready to bring those issues to a much wider audience. As a Chicana, I have been dealing with this for years, it's nothing new. One of the things I have been doing as an artist is learning more about my indigenous roots. Since I couldn't get it in the art departments and I wasn't an anthropology major, I have been studying the ancient history of Mexico on my own. As an artist, this is a very important part, my Indian roots. So it's nothing new, but it gave us a chance to bring the issues out to a wider audience.

Easton: How do you see the activism of today's young Chicano artists, particularly those in the Galería "Regeneration" program, in comparison to what you were doing twenty-five years ago and the path of activism you have taken?

Lomas Garza: It's a different kind of activism. Mostly what they're trying to do is survive as artists, and that's where I feel I can have much more impact, by doing a one-to-one or in small groups. But they're not really that small, there are about thirty artists who have started to meet regularly at the Galería. Then for about three or four of them, I will be giving more direct input. One of them in particular has been interning with me, he's been helping me doing things like filing and learning how to keep records, basically learning the business of art, seeing the kinds of issues that come up in my everyday work, and how I'm handling the situations. There are many different things they need help with.

Easton: So often an artist's involvement with the community is seen as viable only on a big scale, reaching groups instead of individuals.

Lomas Garza: Well you don't get quality time. Because I am so involved with my artwork now, and trying to do as much as I can to produce the work and get it out, especially to a mass audience—I also need to have this more direct impact. It serves my purpose and my needs.

Jennifer Easton is a curator and writer living in Los Angeles.

8

Juan Sanchez

Interviewed by Susan Canning

Of Puerto Rican descent, Juan Sanchez was born in Brooklyn, New York, in 1954. He was inspired to produce works of a political nature by the teachings of the Young Lords, a militant political group modelled after the Black Panthers and dedicated to independence for Puerto Rico, as well as by his teachers, who included Hans Haacke and Leon Golub, and by the Taller Boricua, a Puerto Rican artists' collective. He has continued to investigate issues of political activism and cultural identity and has also organized and curated several shows, including "Ritual and Rhythms: Visual Forces for Survival," at the Kenkeleba House Gallery, New York, and "Beyond Aesthetics: Art of Necessity by Artists of Conscience," at the Henry Street Settlement. Utilizing a technique that combines photographs, found objects, and poetry, Sanchez creates paintings and prints that are reminiscent both of the tangled fragments of the urban milieu and the Puerto Rican home with its portable altars and religious icons. Sanchez uses source material rich with political irony—the once-banned Puerto Rican flag, the credit card that signifies colonial exploitation, the Puerto Rican Day parades that disguise racism and poverty. Addressing his people first and then the general art public, Sanchez does not intend antagonism but enticement: he aims both to instruct and to politicize. Sanchez calls his works "Rican/Structions," works that draw upon the language of art to heal and restore to cultural conscience the vision of those long overlooked by history. This conversation took place in 1990.

Susan Canning: What do you see as the role of political art in the contemporary art world?

Juan Sanchez: Generally speaking, I think that art has a very important role in society. Of course, the dogma pertaining to the whole contemporary art dialogue basically dictates that art and politics don't combine, don't complement, that they should not be together. For some reason it is thought that one takes away from the other and historically speaking that has never been the case. The reality is that art has always been a reflection of society, it's always been a reflection of a particular cultural entity. I think that art, regardless of whether it is figurative and making some kind of sociopolitical statement, or abstract and just playing with the whole formalist concept of art for art's sake, has always served a political function.

For me, 1980 was really the beginning of a critical decade. Things like Art Against Apartheid, Artist's Call Against U.S. Intervention in Central America, and groups like ABC No Rio and Group Material surfaced. These are artists from my generation who at that time were in their early to mid twenties, and just coming out of art school with an incredible fervor and commitment to making social and political statements. I think that this surge of energy was so massive and so strong that the art world had to reckon with it and so in 1980, 1981, 1982 there were an incredible number of political art shows surfacing all over the place. There was an attempt at making statements more from the heart than from the intellect. I think there was an adventure that surfaced from this in terms of experimentation with techniques, concepts, approaches, and states of mind that led to answers to a lot of questions about the relationship art and politics. Of course, there were some very bad answers and some very good answers; but I think that this eventually gave way to artists like Sue Coe or Jenny Holzer and provided a strong platform for people like Nancy Spero or Leon Golub, who before then were well known and respected, but on an underground level. I think the '80s really reinforced and reaffirmed that art and politics are not really separate but that art is politics, that art is about society, about culture, about the rejuvenation and the evolution of humanity.

Canning: What do you think of the relationship between art and the commodity system...how does that relate to art that has a political message? Is it subversive? How does it function once it is bought by the bank and not seen anymore?

Sanchez: That's a very complex question. There was a time when it was very clear what kind of art was purchased through the mainstream art world and supported by corporations. Obviously, abstract art, art that was more pastoral, art that was very conceptualist in its density. It didn't really communicate much as far as the mass public was concerned. If you had some schooling, perhaps you got something out of what that art was trying to say. The Reagan era jolted society in such a way that political art was really surfacing, and then the market had to reckon with that in a certain way. The problem is that if you sell to corporations the subversive function is neutralized in a way. It depends, however, on the context in which that art is used.

My particular concern has always been, considering what I am trying to say in my work, what would happen if a museum were to purchase it and have it in its collection. Considering the fact that the museum becomes a point of reference in terms of credibility, in terms of the superstructure enforcing or defining what is good art or bad art, what is valid or invalid, it almost seems subversive for, say, the Metropolitan, to purchase my work which talks about the question of liberation of a country and about its affinities with other countries in Central America or Latin America. I see that as subversive; just the fact that they purchased the work, even if strictly for its formal merits, gives credibility to what I am trying to say, which, to certain sectors, is very controversial and is a subject that is not really dealt with even among progressives.

At the same time, you have to consider very seriously what kind of political art is entering the mainstream, because there are different levels, different intensities, different statements. The most popular political art at the moment deals with issues which are, literally speaking, outside of this country. It is much easier for people to accept art that is protesting apartheid in South Africa than to deal with art by African-American artists that is also speaking quite loudly, and has been for so many years, about apartheid here in the United States. At the same time, it is very easy for art to have access to the media, the museums, art publications in dealing with the whole struggle in El Salvador, Guatemala, and Nicaragua, but not really deal with the issues of how Chicanos and Puerto Ricans and other Latin Americans here in the United States are struggling against poverty and racism and how that has its affinity to the struggles going on in Latin America. Puerto Rico, for example, is a commonwealth of the United States that is trying to become the fifty-first state of the Union, but the reality is that Puerto Rico has been invaded in the same way that Panama has been invaded recently. It is occupied by the United States forces, it's a colony of the United States. Puerto Rico is so close to home and there are so many of us here in the United States living under poverty that most people would rather not deal with it. They are more comfortable dealing with the Salvadoran poor or the Guatemalan peasants fighting against dictatorship.

Canning: So in a way it's an aspect of liberal guilt...

Sanchez: It's an aspect of liberal guilt but more than anything else it's an aspect of genuine hypocrisy, conscious or unconscious, in which people are not willing to deal with the problems in their own backyards, but then find affinities with the struggles of peoples in other countries. People will rave and protest about social injustice in other countries but they fail to see it within this country.

This aspect compelled me to curate shows myself. In the beginning, when all these political art shows were surfacing, there was always one typical and obvious problem that so many artists of color and people of color have been suffering from, the question of censorship. I would see these shows and I would start counting and ask, well, how many Latinos or African-Americans are in these shows. I began to see that it was mostly the same artists making these statements, and again we felt excluded, censored from making those same statements. I found it very curious, considering the fact that her works are sincere statements that come from a genuine commitment, that someone like Sue Coe would immediately get a platform, much faster than some African-American artist who had been portraying these things from his or her own vantage point. In the first show that I curated in '82, "Beyond Aesthetics: Art of Necessity from Artists of Conscience," I made the point that there had to be a certain number of Latin American, African-American, Asian-American, and white artists, both male and female, to talk about all of these issues that have gone on internationally as well as domestically within the United States. I don't mind artists expressing the plight of Latin-American liberation, but how about letting us Latin Americans in on the protest? It had become this weird thing where Latin America was oppressing people of color and all of a sudden a sector changed its mind. Now they're crying and fighting for our cause, but they still want to be the leaders, they still want to provide the answers, they still want to teach us how to liberate ourselves.

Canning: How does the idea of aesthetic pleasure or beauty, the conventions of formalism relate to the political content? Do you see the "aesthetics of pleasure" as oppositional to art with a political subtext? Does political art have an overriding ideology that doesn't fit with the mainstream view that art should be pleasing and decorative?

Sanchez: We have to begin first with the whole question of the schooling, the indoctrination of the artist. Considering that art schools really promote this whole question of art for art's sake, emphasizing its aesthetic beauty, we cannot help but realize that this view is the dominant index for creating art. What I came to realize is that, not only do art and politics complement each other very well, but to a large extent the aesthetic fitting or complementing the political statement can be very genuine and perhaps even more pure. I feel that what Serrano accomplished and what I am trying to accomplish is far more subversive because the whole idea is to try to get people to look at the work, to appreciate the work for many reasons which are more within their concern. Then you bring forth the real reason that you are creating this kind of work and it becomes more subversive and perhaps manipulative.

I consider myself a kind of formalist. So the whole question of color, the whole question of texture, and the whole dynamic of the formalist attitude of manipulation of pigment and surface is, I feel, ammunition which will entice people who will then have to reckon with what I am trying to say. At the same time, I feel that even if I am talking about terrible things, by using all these formalist vehicles, I am also trying to bring out the beauty of humanity and why we have to protect ourselves and why we have to oppose the inhumanity of man to man. When you go into a museum or gallery you want to see art that is dynamic, wonderful to look at and a great pleasure, because that's what we feel art is. I'll give you that but at the same time, you're going to have to pursue the things that I am trying to say. So it becomes kind of manipulative. It's using a vocabulary that they want, that they are used to responding to, to express some of the terrible things that are happening. It's a way of sensitizing them to these issues.

It's also about a level of intensity and of how you speak to people. So instead of making them avoid you, you make them come closer to you so that they are willing to hear what you have to say.

Canning: So you use the formalist surface to bring people in. It could also be said that you are also introducing the formal beauty of the language of the street (the layers of posters, graffiti, advertisements) and by seeing from this context one can learn to appreciate another point of view, in addition to that art-school-trained understanding of color, shape, etc.

Sanchez: I have to emphasize, however, how much art school and art history try to divorce the lived experience that creates this different type of concept and aesthetic, how they try to divorce art from life, from politics, from society. Throughout the centuries there has always been this evolution as to how to reinterpret, to bring clarity, to bring light to life. So when you're dealing with Impressionism, when you're dealing with Cubism, it's another way to explore lived experience, seeing the physicality of the world and reinterpreting it to bring you in tune with your more spiritual or metaphysical experience. I feel that the dynamics of the street, especially the neighborhoods that I was born and raised in, has a tremendous influence in my work. But I am trying to reinterpret that. I'm trying to reinterpret it in such a way that it can have a more positive and re-evaluating effect. It's not so much about pointing out ugliness and trying to turn it into something beautiful but trying to find within that ugliness the beauty that has allowed us to survive that ugliness. At the same time, in terms of the formalistic approach, I'm not only trying to talk about liberation from the physical chains of political repression and oppression, I'm also trying to elevate consciousness in terms of the psychological and spiritual liberation. I think that people who are not physically chained are still psychologically chained. So the issue is how can I aesthetically deal with the matter to mobilize people to protest, to write, to try to change these things, but at the same time how to spiritually and emotionally bring them to that level where the physical freedom comes.

Canning: You have also included a literary element in your work: words, poetry, your own writing. What do you see as the relationship between the words, the text, and the image in your paintings?

Sanchez: First of all, when we deal with text, with words, we are dealing with markings as opposed to different sign languages or messages. We have a tendency to develop a blind spot to the idea that these letters are marks. These marks have a certain degree of density. They have an incredibly wide range of effect, in the same way that marks used to create an image of a shape or form have. Chinese calligraphy—and we have a tendency to call it calligraphy and not language because we can't read it—has an incredible beauty, a wonderful dynamic to the shapes and forms that we experience them for what they are, for their quality and character. I think that calligraphy has had an incredible effect on us in terms of understanding the sophistication and the intensity of the culture itself.

There is always the problem for me that the language I deal with is Spanish. When I started doing this kind of work I never contemplated it being geared toward an English-speaking society. This work derived from a deficiency and need within my community, to complement a movement, to raise a level of consciousness, and to foster self-empowerment so that people could go out and change the things that are repressing and oppressing them. Language has had an incredible influence on me, especially through songs and Latin American poetry in particular. I would read poems that would talk about liberation and chronicle the history of Puerto Rico against colonialism and imperialism, beginning with Spanish colonialism all the way to United States colonialism. In these poems, metaphors are used to illustrate the atrocity of these things and the plight of strong people fighting against these things.

On the other hand, I use other elements, which as far as I am concerned have a more universal communicating power, like the painted or drawn image as well as the graphic image. I feel that these elements complement and reinforce each other. I have come to realize that when people who do not speak Spanish look at my painting there are other elements that allow them to grapple or deal with the text in a non-literal way, so that the words still have power and influence. In the same way, people may or may not understand one of my paintings in English, but they may understand it and reckon with the language on a different level.

Canning: What about the context and content? Does one need to know the history of Puerto Rico, its colonization, etc., to relate to your work?

Sanchez: I think that those who have some knowledge of the history or culture will certainly get a lot more from the work. I am trying to make statements regarding a particular situation or country, but I am also trying to make a universal connection to other experiences or similar situations. I do not want to function as some kind of objective reporter, but to work in a way that is a reflection of how I react. I think that a lot of the elements in my work have an affinity to Latin American art; viewers have already been introduced to it, so it's only the concrete information about Puerto Rico that they may not know. I hope that people understand enough of my work that they internalize it enough to venture further, to find out what these things are all about. That to me is what education and raising the level of consciousness are all about.

Susan Canning is an arts writer living in New York.

9

Conrad Atkinson

Interviewed by Penelope Shackelford

Conrad Atkinson is a painter and conceptual artist whose work has been at the forefront of the "interventionist" style of political art. His work has ranged from installations to posters, welcome mats, metal constructions, newspaper parodies, and magazine covers (including the cover of Art Papers' *"Interventionist" issue, January/February, 1990). His work addresses both broad and very specific political and social issues, as well as the politics of the art world. He has also often examined the historical context of his own West Cumbria roots in England, which was a key site in the origins of both the labor movement and Romantic poetry, as well as the setting for* Wuthering Heights. *His work has been widely exhibited and written about, and is in the permanent collections of the Tate Gallery, the British Museum, and the Victoria and Albert Museum in England, the Museum of Modern Art and the Brooklyn Museum in the United States, and the Australian National Gallery. As he discusses in the following conversation, his art has demonstrated a rare capacity to achieve a direct impact on public discourse and social action, without deviating from the formal and intellectual seriousness that has always characterized Atkinson's work. He has been an inspiration to many artists who have adopted interventionist tactics. The interview was conducted in 1994.*

Penelope Shackelford: Do you have a "mission" in your work?

Conrad Atkinson: No. It sounds too religious for me. I have certain beliefs and goals that are pursued. Is art autonomous or is it inevitably entwined in the fabric of everything we do? Some people argue that painting, sculpture, etc. are autonomous, that they are not connected in any way with our other belief systems. They can quite happily paint pictures, make sculptures, and so on without being concerned with what happens with them when they go out of the studio or what the audience for them would be, or that people are starving or whatever. It is quite a difficult question to resolve because you get somebody like Joseph Beuys who says, "If I speak, it's art." Someone such as Robert Rauschenberg says, "I paint my pictures, they go into the world and I have no more control over them and I don't even think about them. I paint them for myself." And then you get into the problem of the definitions of what is art. Duchamp would say, "If I say it's art, it's art." Carl Andre would say something such as, "I'm an artist, that's what I do; sometimes it's good art; sometimes it's bad art. I'm an artist." Other people would say that art sounds like a definition of quality. Basically, all the methods of art are crafts. When a craft is carried to its highest level and the physical, emotional, and intellectual fuse, then it becomes art in my opinion, but there are many different notions of what art is. Some people would prefer not to talk about art at all, but prefer to talk about culture and the production of culture. Art has come to signify precious objects that have a high monetary value. It has come to signify personal expression as well. If you talk about culture as the production of meaning, everything else changes.

One can't avoid making meanings. The problem is that some of the meanings may be racist or sexist or contain a million other attitudes. It's the analysis of the meanings that one makes and it is that kind of dynamic between meaning and all the other things one could feel. That's the problem. It's not the technique. I learned the craft of painting and I can do that extremely well or I could at one point—well enough to get an honors degree from the Royal Academy Schools. It's not about the craft; it's more about the production of meaning.

Shackelford: Joseph Beuys said that "To have radical change in the social structure, one needs a highly developed philosophy and ways of production in the art world."

Atkinson: I have a great number of problems with Beuys. I knew him a little and I miss him, but I think there was a lot of mystification in his stance. What is significant about his achievement is the way in which he situated himself between what might be called the art of politics or the art of social action. I don't think his politics were very radical in many ways. I like most the creative variety of his positioning of himself in relation to the art world and its use as his vehicle and stage. For someone like me the problem that Beuys didn't address is the way in which one actually inserts oneself in the ruling hegemony and in a popular mode at the same time. How can you operate in a New York art gallery and in a mining village in the north of England at the same time? It raises all the problems of audience, media, accessibility, imagery, history, culture, and all of that. The main problem for my generation is trying to bridge that gap between art and life. It wasn't a problem that Beuys had because he was of an earlier generation.

Shackelford: Your work creates an environment in which people can see how to make choices. In this sense the work is functionally transformative.

Atkinson: When I did *Strike*, a number of members of the left said, "This is a wonderful exhibition. This actually shows you that art can do something material." It unionized a factory and it changed people's lives. That's a double-edged weapon because once you start laying on artists that they have to materially transform the physical situation of somebody else or the world, then you expect too much of an artwork. You have to say, well yes. I did intend things to happen as a result of the exhibition. The way in which I structured it allowed things to happen.

Shackelford: So the structural process leading up to the exhibit was as important as the exhibit?

Atkinson: The physical bit where it was on the walls temporarily was part of a whole long series of interactions. In preparation for *Strike*, there were meetings, discussions, this or that. Then the exhibition happened and there were meetings in the exhibition with members of Parliament and government ministers. The exhibition in the gallery concluded, but it continued on.

The photographs of the workers went back into the housing projects from where the workers had come. They are now hanging on those walls. Some bits went into public art collections. There were immediate things going on at the same time. This was a long time ago. It was in 1972 and felt like a very strange thing to do for an artist. There are two things going on here: one is the material transformation. Once one has dismissed satirizing, picturing a whole range of imageries of a particular situation, then one has to say, "Is there something else I can do, can that situation be changed, could that be my function in this one?" But that doesn't mean to say that that's what I'm always going to do. You can see the problems when I go to Northern Ireland and *The Guardian* has a headline—"Atkinson Goes to Northern Ireland"—and then starts off by saying, "He unionized the workers in a factory in his last exhibition. Now we expect great things from him in Northern Ireland." Well, that's crazy. That's too much to ask of any artwork or exhibition or any single individual including a government minister. The expectations become disproportionate to what art can supply. There is a myth that says that art can transform things instantly. One painting can't do that. Occasionally, accidents of history make certain paintings the flashpoint for something, for example, *The Raft of the Medusa* by Gericault, which became the symbol of the inability of the French regime to adapt to change. It became a kind of liberal flag, but one that didn't picture the storming of the barricades; it depicted a raft from a sunken ship. The content and the imagery in the painting didn't correspond to the political impact that it had. The same thing, on a smaller scale, happened with my picture called *Silver Liberties*. It was painted in 1977, when the queen's silver jubilee was on. It was at the same time that we were before the European Court of Human Rights for the worst abuses of civil liberties in the so-called civilized world in Northern Ireland. I painted an Irish flag with various things on it and it was exhibited in London in an exhibition called "Art for Society." It was hung in the same place, the Whitechapel Gallery, that Jasper Johns's American flag had been hung several years previously. When it went over to Northern Ireland, it became a kind of political flashpoint.

There were crowds of people outside the gallery with banners saying, "Get this picture down." There were questions in the House of Commons and Lords about this picture. Eventually it was removed and put somewhere else. As a result, the Ulster Museum's trustees resigned. That's an example of a picture that has political content and becomes a political situation in itself. But it's too much to ask of every artwork, that it can do all that stuff as well as carry cultural, economic, and ideological messages. To get back to the function business, asking for material change in an existing physical situation is something that is too much to hang on any individual or any artist. Nevertheless, it did at that particular time contradict the kind of classical Marxist notion that the economic base simply determines the superstructure. In other words, economics is the base and everything is reflected directly from the base. He who pays the piper calls the tune. What I was arguing against is that one can't reduce things to their economic determinants. Although there is a complicated way through that will show that economics is a major factor. The notion of art being a strategic and tactical activity was new because in the '60s, people just painted pictures and hung them on walls. That's an oversimplification but basically that's it. The idea that art had a series of strategies and tactics and directed itself to different audiences, and could take different forms was new. Furthermore, an awareness that came partly from the women's movement was that certain forms had been privileged forms. Paintings, for example, were usually large, flat, square, and American and were being presented as universal, disinterested, objective great art.

Shackelford: Ignoring the other.

Atkinson: Ignoring everything else. In 1972 there was a lot of very cool, conceptual work from people such as The Art and Language Group with no recognition of political realities. Although they would have argued that what they were doing was political art, I saw it just as more of the avant-garde. My work came out of the streets in the sense of the grassroots level. As opposed to that, there was a kind of abstract expressionist thing and a post-pop thing going on as well. So when

Strike happened that polarized a lot of opinion very strongly. Even people who thought themselves to be politically sophisticated thought it was crass and vulgar.

Shackelford: Art often starts out in the public interest and later ends up as a commodity. How can an artist criticize the system and still distribute work through the agents of the system such as mainstream, highbrow galleries?

Atkinson: There are a couple of things: where could I go to be outside the system? The other thing is that there are many different discourses and struggles. They happen at different levels and for different lengths of time. There is no longer one enemy to which we can point. You have to occupy the ruling hegemonic spaces as well as popular areas. Otherwise, you render yourself invisible. We also have to pick up on this term "political art." There really isn't such a thing. All art has a political as well as an aesthetic, ideological, cultural, and economic dimension. All of those things interact at different points of insertion as a tactic in an overall strategy. For example, if I didn't show in a New York gallery, you wouldn't be interviewing me now. I know friends of mine who changed the focus in the late '60s and early '70s who haven't done projects in *Artforum* and *Art in America*, haven't been interviewed, haven't been on TV, haven't had programs made on them. Consequently, their work isn't being taught in art schools. They are completely invisible in the ruling discourse and hegemony. Their work is lost for a generation; it's not being fed into the art schools. Their tactics at that time were wrong, I thought. I told them they were wrong, they told me I was wrong. They said I shouldn't be doing work in the community, in newspapers, in New York galleries. The choice was presented as a stark one in the earlier '70s. There was a lot of black-and-whiteness. I strongly argued against ghettoizing ourselves into any situation like that. The bottom line is basically flexible tactics and rock-hard principles.

Shackelford: You can't work outside the system.

Atkinson: There is no outside.

Shackelford: The gallery is also a forum for the dissemination of ideas.

Atkinson: You could argue that in the gallery system there is an intellectual discourse. It doesn't have a direct material effect on people's lives. It doesn't help to get compensation for lung disease like the miners' strike did. *Das Kapital* is not floating around on the shop floor in factories. It's a quite complicated piece of work by Marx. It's not enough to say that the work just has to go to the factory floor or to the community. It actually has to do other things as well.

Shackelford: Such as?

Atkinson: Because we're talking about culture which is a complicated mechanism there are no correct solutions. It can't be politically correct. If you look at some of the politically correct pictures from Soviet Russia or anywhere else for that matter and you look from a 1994 perspective and try to see what the world view was then, its a profoundly reactionary role. If you look at works from the '60s and '70s and you try to see the role of gay men or gay women in them you'll find that they are not there, they're absent. Anybody who thinks that they know what is politically correct is mistaken. That's why I coined that little sequence of phrases, "You never know when you're gonna need culture, you never know where culture is gonna come from, you never know what culture is for, you never know what it's gonna do and you never know when you're gonna come up against it." Any group that tells you the correct line to take is almost inevitably wrong because in 1994 there are no correct solutions.

Shackelford: You've spoken of the political power of art as affecting every level of life. Does the NEA have a responsibility towards that power?

Atkinson: The NEA differs from a number of funding bodies in other countries such as the Australian Council, the Canada Council, the Arts Council of Great Britain, the French Ministry of Culture. Among these groups the theory is that it's a disinterested body that hands out money to the best art. The NEA needs to be protected from the politicians of the world. It has an influence disproportionate to its money. The amount of money it has is absolute peanuts. It doesn't make an iota of difference to the art world in that sense.

Shackelford: Its role is symbolic.

Atkinson: It's symbolic, but it should also show leadership. It should ideally be the place where the discourse on the culture of the nation is democratically argued and is subject to all the pressures that any democracy is subject to. But in fact it's not that simple, because it is under a disproportionate amount of pressure. President Clinton should restructure the NEA and render it arm's length from central government. He should also consider creating a Ministry of Culture which will make most Americans throw their hands up in horror because they'll say didn't Stalin have one of those and I'll say yes, but so did France under Jack Lang. He did wonderful things. The first British Minister of Culture, Jenny Lee, wasn't exactly a minister of culture, but her portfolio managed to develop an interesting number of things and protect the agency from politicians. The way forward that I can see for the NEA and public funding is to do it with what is called "the arm's length principle" in some countries. It means that the agency is kept at arm's length from political decisions. It has good things and bad things in it, but what it means is that, for example, in Great Britain, you can't ask questions in the House of Commons about specific things that the Arts Council of Great Britain has done. That's the theory anyway. The whole thing needs to be restructured. It's completely impossible as I see it right now.

Shackelford: Now that you are living in California, is it possible to deal with American culture in the way that you deal with British culture?

Atkinson: To a certain extent, I won't be dealing with the problems that I dealt with in Britain. In a sense I see myself as opening up things. There are certain things here that fascinate me. You can't be in California without being aware of Hollywood. I am looking at Hollywood as an important cultural institution that has a major affect on the whole world. That's my current thing. I'll also go looking at nationalism because the United States is interesting in terms of its position on imperialism and nationalism. I spent some time in eastern Europe and Russia so I'm quite interested in that area. A ten-year-old work of mine, *For Wordsworth, For West Cumbria*, has just been exhibited. By coincidence, it has a reference to immigration to California. It was put in long before I knew I would be immigrating to California. It's in the context of a poem by a miner from my part of the country in the 1880s. I'll be developing the themes of migration and immigration as well as nationalism.

Shackelford: Related to this is your interest in Emily Brontë's *Wuthering Heights* as well as the works of Wordsworth and Shelley.

Atkinson: We spoke earlier of times to be overtly political and times not to be ideological. I was invited to do a show by the Henry Moore Sculpture Trust in England and I decided to do an installation on *Wuthering Heights*. This was an attempt to launder my image into a romantic English poet. It didn't really work because as soon as you start digging into *Wuthering Heights* all these things come up.

Shackelford: It portrays the darkest side of man.

Atkinson: Yes, but look what Hollywood made of it.

Shackelford: An epic love story.

Atkinson: Your universal, in other words. So, in a sense you are answering your own question. There is no universal. Incidentally, Merle Oberon, who played Cathy, was born in India of an Indian mother and a Scottish father. When she came to Hollywood, she passed her mother off as an Indian servant rather than acknowledge the truth. The film itself, which is supposed to be the English classic love story, has dark elements. The whole structure of the classic English romance breaks down when we examine the fact that Heathcliff probably could have been black or Irish. At one point Nelly Dean says to him, "Who knows but your mother was an Indian princess and your father a Chinese king?" He's talked of as a dark thing muttering strange language and referred to as a gypsy. His race is questionable. Cathy and Heathcliff never get married because there is a reading that says that Cathy is the feminine side of Emily Brontë and Heathcliff is the masculine side. There are also hints of anorexia read throughout the text. Anorexia is usually a sign of abuse by the father. Emily's father was a fundamentalist preacher. He taught her manly pursuits—shooting and so on. She was the first generation daughter of a fundamentalist, immigrant preacher from Ireland. All the girls spoke with quite a strong Irish accent up until they were well into their teens. In that area of Halifax now, there are a lot of women Emily's age from Bangladesh. It was where the Rushdie affair exploded and *Satanic Verses* was burned. These women who many people wouldn't think were English, especially the right wing in England, are as English as Emily Brontë. So even when I try to do something nice, it becomes a struggle.

Shackelford: David Thompson describes Northern England as the place where the modern economies were founded: the Joint Stock Act in 1844 is the basis for the modern stock corporation; the same year Marx wrote *The German Ideology*; Engels was based in Manchester when he wrote *The Conditions of the Working Class in England* in 1844. The roots of these movements form the historical basis from which much of your own work springs.

Atkinson: Also, Emily was writing *Wuthering Heights* in 1844. The material conditions of the time affect Howarth where Emily Brontë lived. Howarth is always presented as an isolated village way out in the fells; it was actually a highly industrialized town at the heart of the industrial revolution. It had the highest mortality rate in Great Britain, apart from sections of London. Emily was confronted by these deaths all the time as the daughter of a vicar. The average life expectancy was twenty-five. Her work is based on the material conditions of the time. She wasn't an isolated, dreaming romantic, just as Wordsworth and Shelley weren't in the generation before her. Shelley said that artists are the unacknowledged legislators of the world. When he wrote "Queen Mab," which is about family, feminism, law, and patriarchy, poetry was an elitist and dying minority art form: he printed it in an edition of 200. Twenty years later, there were 20,000 copies of this poem in the pockets of the first Chartists (the early Labor Unionists) when they were marching in Trafalgar Square and other places. That is a work in an elitist form that suddenly became very accessible. You never know where culture is going to come from. There are a number of myths about the Romantic, detached artist living in the country isolated from politics, events, and reality which aren't true. They were living in the cradle of the industrial revolution. Likewise, in many parts of the world today many more artists are realizing a social dimension. One has to ask oneself, how long does a work of art last before it becomes something else? Time scales are variable. Even now in West Cumbria one would be near the site of the world's first nuclear power station. One would be heavily involved in contemporary issues. It's not as heavily populated now as it was then, but one couldn't help observing the nuclear power station and how it fits into the rest of the world. One has to relate it to Chernobyl, Three Mile Island, and so on. Art is oppositional. When it is easily acceptable, it produces academies. Academies produce art that serves the ends and aspirations of that society, and that's perfectly normal. You can say, "What about the abstract expressionists? Weren't they rebels and opposed to American capitalism?" That's true, if one sees their work as an intervention against what they began to see as the increasing constraints of social realism through the '30s and the WPA. Then the work is appropriated by the state, it's contextualized, then it's sent to Viet Nam to show the people what they are missing. The picture that Jackson Pollock painted is not the one you are looking at. This also confronts the notion of great art being eternal or universal. Raphael was buried for centuries and only resuscitated recently. Different artists have different levels of acceptance at different periods of time. Art isn't great forever and all the time. Imagine if the Chinese economy becomes the superpower of the world and the U.S. withers away. Do you think the most famous artist in China will be Jackson Pollock? No. We're talking about strategy and tactics. But that's not to say there isn't great art.

Shackelford: You once said that many artists had gone into teaching in order to save themselves even though teaching was not so good for them. But now here you are in California teaching and chairing a major art department. Have things changed?

Atkinson: I wanted a change and I had a long connection with the States, mostly the East Coast. For a number of reasons we felt that now was the time to change, because of our children and so on. When we investigated coming here without being affiliated with any institution it looked difficult. To be affiliated with an institution gave us a community right away. I also thought it was a good opportunity to try and build an art school from one that had a great reputation but had lost a lot of faculty and was looking for a direction.

Shackelford: How would you respond to the critics who say you confine the meaning of art to social practice and conceptualism?

Atkinson: All art work is conceptual, social, political, and ideological. The skill is in knowing what subjects to tackle and where to tackle them, on what scale to tackle them, and where to insert them into the cultural debate of our society. That's where the skill lies, and it doesn't matter whether it's a painting, a text, a banner, a postcard, a video, a spoken word piece, cassette, whatever. After you have achieved the craft skills of drawing, painting, and editing, the skills become less important. What I objected to about the '60s was that it closed down options for artists. Before the '60s, artists had done a whole range of stuff from books to murals. Most artists would accept most commissions and adapt themselves. In the '60s there was an intense focus on the white box in New York, in which to show stuff. That distorted art and its possibilities. It's not wrong to do that, but that's only one narrow option. I think also you will have to forgive me for saying there is a certain confused, dated parochialism about such critiques, if you are talking about my critics. There is no longer a problem between conceptual art and painting, any more than there is a problem between abstraction and figuration. These are old arguments dead a long time ago. It's depressing. In a lot of art practice, there is confusion about the notion of art as an object that's for sale. There is nothing wrong with that. Artists are material beings, they have to earn a living. But when you confuse that with the production of meaning, then there is a problem. There is a lot of confectionery that presents itself as real painting or sculpture.

Shackelford: How does the activism of today's art differ from the activism of twenty years ago?

Atkinson: Twenty years ago you weren't supposed to do anything outside of hanging the stuff on the walls. Now there are many more groups you can relate to, many more you can do research with, many more organized alternative groups. There are more battered women's groups, industrial disease groups. Almost all of these things are now on the agenda, whereas they weren't then. We didn't have a language for dealing with it. When I did *Strike* in 1971 I felt completely isolated, but it would have sat quite nicely in the Whitney show in 1993.

Shackelford: Is it time to drop the word art?

Atkinson: It's very useful in Western civilization even though it makes me very uncomfortable to be called an artist, because it seems like a quality judgment.

Shackelford: What would you call yourself?

Atkinson: The jargon would be "cultural worker," but that's as complicated as the word artist. It's such a loaded term and so constraining. There are people who think that because they pick up a paint brush and put paint on canvas, they're artists. They're painters; they may be artists, they may not be, but that's something else. I think it's a useful term right now because it gives you certain permissions psychologically. I am going to a conference in a few weeks' time which is dealing with interdisciplinary issues, those not grabbed by any discipline yet, in which nobody knows what it's about and where it's going. These are art practices that occupy the cracks in what is an increasingly homogenized civilization. So "artist" is a useful word in that context, because approach, medium, and subject matter are so fluid.

***Penelope Shackelford** is a freelance writer and art critic living in Davis, California.*

10

Fred Wilson

Interviewed by Curtia James

*Fred Wilson's best known installations critique museums and museology,
but his work also gives voice to the stories of individuals silenced by racism
and colonialism. Wilson does not simply speak for them, he finds ways to
bring these individuals forward to speak for themselves. Wilson creates
mixed media installations that often use material drawn from museum
collections (often seldom-discussed holdings) in provocative juxtapositions,
using both humor and disturbing insights: African masks are gagged with
foreign flags, slave shackles contrasted with silver trays, a volume on
African art is pressed under the weight of a statue exalting tomes on
Western art history. His best known installation thus far has been "Mining
the Museum," an exhibition sponsored by Baltimore's The Contemporary
and the Maryland Historical Society (for a detailed discussion of this work,
see "Installing History" by curator Lisa G. Corrin in* Art Papers,
*July/August, 1994). For a retrospective exhibition at North Carolina's
Southeastern Center for Contemporary Art (SECCA) in 1994, Wilson also
created new works, "Old Salem: A Family of Strangers," an exhibit of dolls
culled from Old Salem's collection and a series of installations at the Old
Salem village in Winston-Salem, where SECCA is located, and "Insight:
In Site: In Sight: Incite: Memory," which encompassed images of displace-
ment, family, community, and racial strife. Wilson researched the project
for several months, relying on Old Salem's resources as well as those of the
Museum of Early Southern Decorative Arts, Winston-Salem State
University's Society for the Study of Afro-American History, Delta Fine
Arts, historians and Winston-Salem's black community. The nineteenth-
century German-speaking Moravians of Old Salem were meticulous record
keepers, which made Wilson's findings particularly fruitful. The following
discussion of Wilson's work, which took place in 1990, focuses particularly
on the Old Salem installations, but also provides insights into Wilson's
motivation and process, as well as the power of all his work to evoke
previously invisible communities.*

Curtia James: How did the exhibition at SECCA come about?

Fred Wilson: It seemed an extension of what I had done in Baltimore. I am interested in historic villages and how they construct their realities, how they construct the past. My interests lie in how museums construct meanings, and historic villages do this on a larger scale.

Also, my grandfather's buried there and his second wife lives down there, and I hadn't seen her in twenty-four years. So it was really intriguing to me to find this side of my family, which I knew very very little about. My father is an international consulting engineer who lives in Spain, and he didn't have addresses or anything because I believe the last time he was there was for my grandfather's funeral. My sister had been to North Carolina. But for some reason I hadn't been. And, in these situations, there's always trepidation—you're not sure they're going to like you.

James: How did you find them?

Wilson: I had somebody do some research and found my grandfather's burial plot. I talked about it with a lot of people. Susan Lubowsky [Executive Director of SECCA] explained the situation at one of her board meetings and said, "Fred's family is here, and here are their names." And someone said, "I know who that is. I know his son." They gave me the number of my stepgrandmother. She was very hesitant at first because my name is rather common. After that she was just great. It just was one of those things. If I hadn't met the board member I would have still been searching around.

James: How do you approach installations like "Panta Rhei: A Gallery of Ancient Classical Art" at the biennial at Cairo, and "Mining the Museum" in Baltimore?

Wilson: It depends on the exhibition and how I react to the material. Then the information just flows through me. The exhibition in Baltimore also looked at African-American history and the denial by the museum culture of the intensity of that experience. For me, it's a matter of letting the floodgates flow in terms of the information, and my reaction to reading the information and seeing the things in the collection that were not being exhibited.

The show in Egypt created an environment where there was a literal dialogue between the Egyptians and the rest of the world—I had Egyptian voices and European voices emanating from pots and other things that I included in the installation. I'd lived in Egypt many years ago with my father, and that left a deep impression on me. I felt very comfortable there. So the piece was really about how the West views Egypt. Europeans have claimed them and African Americans have claimed them, but Egyptians essentially think of themselves as Egyptians. They've been there for millennia and other people come to see what they do but essentially they are who they are.

When I go into a project, I'm not looking to bring something to it. I'm responding more than anything else. I get feelings about things. I'm not thinking, "What can I do that is different from things done before?" You can still get a very personal emotional response from a situation or an individual who lived a hundred years ago. It's connecting over time that I'm responding to. The historical information shifts and changes. People have a range of emotions that are fairly steadfast so pain can be felt from one person to another or through generations. In that way it's another kind of connection that's as real or as tangible as any date.

The installation at Old Salem was much more abstract than other things that I have worked with. It was good for me to see the range of things that I can do. Also just being in Winston-Salem, meeting the family and getting a sense of what this part of the South is about and to be in a religious community was a good experience for me.

James: Because I work at Colonial Williamsburg, I'm familiar with slave artifacts and quarters, which prepared me for those you chose at Old Salem. But how have the objects you gathered for the Vogler House and subsequent installation at Old Philips Church been received by the public?

Wilson: Extremely well. It's been quite a phenomenon. It has been an emotional experience for the black community there. One day when I was there, I came to the church to open up and there were some flowers left on the steps. The piece was very much about the black Moravians who lived and worked in Old

Salem, and while Old Salem had done lots of research on the black Moravians and had written a couple of pamphlets and had a slide show about them, the fact that there were Africans at that site was not on the mind of the black community or represented at Old Salem to a great degree. This project breathed life into the blacks who lived there. This, I think, was a very powerful experience for people coming to visit.

James: How receptive were the white Moravians to your efforts?

Wilson: They understand that this is a history that's going to be told. They were just concerned about how it was told and that it was fair. They were afraid that contextually this would be out of whack. I found people very responsive. I gave a lecture to the interpreters and they all came in costume. I had a hard time seeing them as contemporary people.

One never knows how people are going to respond to your work. You're not thinking about the public when you're doing your work. You're reaching out at the public through who you are. You're doing this exploration for yourself with the hope that you will reach others as well. So the response of the public was a completely pure one, it thrills me that we have made that connection through this art work. The thought that someone left flowers at the church door—I never would have thought of that. That is really the joy of that particular piece for me.

James: I immediately connected with the importance of the Bible, which was a mainstay for some within the slave community. But what beyond the obvious did you hope to convey by using the leather whip?

Wilson: I wanted to make specific reference to the abuse and the fact that there was this whip around. I just felt compelled to use it. They actually did use it in their slide presentation that the public sees. But it's not talked about too much. It is such a lightning rod. I placed it with the Bible and called them both *Leather Bound*. They were bound by the abuse of slavery and bound by the religion of the Moravians.

That's why I like using first-hand documentation because it's irrefutable. It's there. Often I try to avoid religion in my work because religion is so subjective, but I felt I had to deal with the subject because it was there. There was truth in this. The church probably was a safe haven, but it was a haven with a price.

James: Why did you include blue medical glasses?

Wilson: I saw them, and there was something about the design of them—I thought they were absolutely beautifully made. Rather than ignore them because there was no connection, I just went with it. As an artist you have to go with things sometimes. Realizing that I was attracted to blue, I had to put blue in the church as well. The blue spotlights in the church, like the two lenses, cast light in the large church and on the houses and the pews and the space in general to give it a certain kind of atmosphere. And I just decided it had to be blue and the blue started with those glasses. The glasses were for protection, and the church was for protection. When I looked through them, they made things look beautiful. It was a way for me to access that feeling of protection. Remarkably, some people actually saw that, they saw the relation. It was really something that I just felt rather than said. Feelings are as true as anything else. All the time we're using them to shore up our visual and intellectual reference. I try to bring the other senses in where it makes sense, the sense of touch, the sense of smell, the sense of hearing, and also emotions and just how you can feel things in your body, not just in your head. Often I try to bring these other references to my work because those are things that are left out of the museum experience. If you look at other societies around the globe, those other senses are really important. How your body reacts to certain objects and things plays a role in how we understand the world. So I work with those tools.

James: One of the diary accounts mentions that one Moravian man asked another to whip his female slave because he was too tired to do so himself. The casualness of the deal seemed sad and absurd to me. How did reading such accounts affect you?

Wilson: What's so frightening about these entries is that they're so offhand, so matter-of-fact. The one thing about history, if you really get involved with it and think about it in a broad way, is, how will future generations view us and what are we taking for granted and what are we speaking about matter-of-factly in our general lives that our future will bear out?

James: How, as a black man, has working so extensively with the subject of slavery changed you personally?

Wilson: Prior to doing the Baltimore show I had really not touched on the subject of slavery in my work. My work was largely about colonialism, largely about Africa and other issues of the nineteenth century. When I was invited to Baltimore, I chose that particular institution. I was not interested in making work that had anything to do with victimization. But of course going through the materials there, I chose the institution because I felt the tension in my body. Here was a museum about Maryland history, with a vast gap and a lot of things unspoken about African-American history. And I came to realize it wasn't just African-American or Native-American history but it was the history of anyone who wasn't white America. Actually it's all there, but it's veiled and homogenized to reflect the history of elite Maryland. And I felt this denial kept them from really understanding Maryland history. People who go there either buy into it or don't feel a part of it.

James: Tell me why you chose to use the silhouettes on the lawn in front of the church and throughout the town as the third part of your installation.

Wilson: There were silhouettes all over Old Salem in the storage vaults. I had silhouettes made of local people in Happy Hill, the black neighborhood where the slaves lived who worked in Old Salem, which continues to be a black community. I was really interested in these connections. I didn't want to do a project that was insular to Old Salem, but I wanted to connect Old Salem to other communities, including the black community. I wanted to connect them to historic architecture that wasn't connected with blacks.

I had silhouettes made of different people to represent those blacks who were Moravians in the 1800s and placed the silhouettes on the lawn of the church. Then to show the slaves' presence, throughout the town, I also placed these silhouettes around the buildings to say how many blacks there were there.

That prompted questions that the various shop owners had to answer about the former black population. It's not that they don't want to talk about the subject. They know they don't know enough. They just have to get past that type of fear.

James: Once I entered the church, it seemed that suddenly everything started to change. What was familiar went awry, with an element of sadness closing in at every point. Susan Lubowsky told me that the guides at Old Salem were taken aback when some visiting the installation would cry. They simply were not used to people having such emotional responses on their tours. Was this an emotional experience for you?

Wilson: The whole project was an emotional and a spiritual experience. Getting deeply involved in the material, the emotions well up in you. What really had an emotional response for me was developing a connection with my family. One became analogous to the other and personalized for me the research of the Moravians—that quest for knowing something that perhaps you never knew, finding emotions that you never had, meeting people that you couldn't possibly have known.

James: What led you to incorporate headstones from Old Salem's collection?

Wilson: I saw the headstones before I began gathering anything else. When I saw them, I was amazed. When I spoke with these researchers, very little information was given. I felt I wanted to give life to these people. I wanted people to think about these individuals before they even got to the church and to think about the church in a much more tangible way—that these people are real, that you could reach out and touch them.

James: What was the significance of the handmade shoes?

Wilson: You do these things and you realize why you did it later. I knew that that space right there was an important space. Originally I carved the word "FREEDOM" in the dirt. I placed the shoes there because to me handmade shoes are like a person. There's something about them that is really alive. I felt they were like a person. They were also floating above the ground because they were on these beams. I was thinking about having someone greet you, who's in between those two states.

James: I was struck by the gourds you chose to use in the former schoolroom in the church. Why did you make this particular choice?

Wilson: There was an abundance of them. I responded directly to their shapes. They're about growth. It's about something alive and growing. This connection to Africa was something that I didn't expect people to see. On a formal level, balancing these things on the beams and then you go to the other space and you see the houses balanced on the beams—it makes a formal connection. Placing these things on the beams gives it a floor without being a floor. They're hovering. Without them there you just focus on the dirt, the earth. They're of the earth and they're not in the earth. The graves were right beneath the floor where people were worshipping.

James: The hymns brought back so many memories for me, but I listened in the setting you'd created as though I was hearing them for the first time. How did you capture them?

Wilson: I asked the Moravian Church if they would allow me to come to come tape their services. Using the white Moravian church that is on the site at Old Salem made their connection to the project a little stronger.

James: On the narratives, over and over I heard an older voice saying, "I don't know," or "I don't remember" to a child's questions about the buildings. Whose voices were you re-creating?

Wilson: The child asks various questions of her grandmother: "Were they safe here/were they happy here/how did it smell/how did it sound," and her grandmother says, "I don't remember, I don't remember," kind of lovingly. Before I came down, I saw my grandmother a lot. She's ninety-seven and she's very active. Once I asked her, "Did you know Romare Bearden?" She said, "I don't know." And I described him, and she said, "You mean Little Romey?"

More recently, since I knew I was going down to Winston-Salem, I asked her about the houses, and she said, "I don't remember." And it really struck me. If I had asked her five years ago she would have remembered. It felt like that's gone and it was a mournful feeling and I should have tried to connect with her, and I should have tried to ask her earlier. We sort of take it for granted that we can access information about our family, but the fact is that we need to get it while we can. At St. Philips I was trying to capture the sadness that I had.

Curtia James *is a Williamsburg, Virginia-based freelance writer. This interview was funded in part by the Center for Arts Criticism in St. Paul, Minnesota, with a grant from the National Endowment for the Arts.*

11

Kathy Acker

Interviewed by Jay Murphy

Kathy Acker is one of the most daring and innovative novelists writing today. She is the author of Blood and Guts in High School; Great Expectations; My Death, My Life, by Pier Paolo Pasolini; Empire of The Senseless; My Mother: A Demonology; *and* Pussy, King of the Pirates, *among others. She also wrote the script for the film* Variety, *and has recently collaborated with the band Mekons on a CD project. Her fictional technique combines plagiarism, pornography, postmodern pastiche, and an autobiographical voice that cries aloud the pains, injustices, and fleeting pleasures of contemporary life. She has also frequently written art criticism and theory, and her work has been associated as often with the work of contemporary visual and performance artists as with literary artists. Her work has obvious affinities with the interventionist tactics of the Situationists of the '50s and '60s (whose work has often been revived in the past twenty years), but Acker has often made fun of the revolutionary poses adopted by the Situationists and the Baudrillardians of later decades. Her own work seeks a more subterranean, feminist, and ambisexual intervention into the moral and normative structures that continue to limit the scope of human life. In 1986, at the time of this interview, Acker was living in England. Kathy Acker died November, 1997.*

Jay Murphy: How do you respond to feminist critics who say that you continue the tradition of woman-as-victim, that you are a woman who writes in a misogynist voice?

Kathy Acker: Well, I think there is a big debate going on in feminism as regards my work. I don't think that it's about woman-as-victim. According to feminist ideals, when you write you're supposed to have a model of the perfect woman, and that's not really what writing is about for me. When I write I have a problem, and depending on what the problem is, say victims, I take a lot of texts. In one text from *Empire of the Senseless*, I was interested in what it was to be male, so I took three different texts by men about what it was like to be male, and put them together.

If I had moralized, or if I had an idea of what I wanted to say, it would have prevented me from finding out things. The school of feminism that would be very angry at me for what I do (I don't want to say typically feminist, I would like to think there are at least two schools of feminism) would probably want me to moralize. They would want me to say, "Men are this way; oh, this is not right." First of all, that sets up a very funny relationship of author to reader; it's definitely a moralistic stance, a very elitist one. It also prevents one from finding out anything, whereas for me the purpose of writing, the reason I write, is to find out things. And I'm not finding out anything if I start out with a prejudgment.

Murphy: So a lot of the examination of sado-masochism is exploring the way people actually are.

Acker: It's different from text to text and it's not all that innocent, to be honest. There is a level of fascination—I usually write about things I'm fascinated with. There's either something I hate or really love; there's some sort of emotion I'm trying to reach.

Murphy: As in a catharsis?

Acker: No, not catharsis, interest. Maybe there is catharsis involved, maybe not, but there is a great deal of obsession. I'm trying to break through—"How does that work? That is the weirdest thing I ever read—why? Why does that go on?" I'm fascinated with a certain power connection and then I'll work through it. Power is often a concern of mine and sometimes when I want to figure out how something is happening or works I'll take texts about the world and it ends up that women are portrayed as victims. You see, if I had just said that, in a feminist tract, "women are victims"—that is almost pap at this point. People get very angry because the material in my texts, as opposed to, say, a Jackie Collins book, or even Kristeva's work, is very direct. I'm just putting it down and I'm not moralizing. Certainly I'm not portraying a woman as victim, I'm showing that that is the portrayal, and that's shocking, right? When we read porn in Jackie Collins it isn't shocking. When we are saying, "Hey, look at what we're reading, and we don't even think about it"—that's shocking. I've had to analyze why people are so shocked by material they see in a lot of places. To say that women are victims in my work, well they're not, not if you look at every female figure.

Now there's another element which I think adds to the confusion. I use the word sado-masochism solely about a consensual relationship between two people; I'm not using it to equal a social relationship in the world—rape, murder, anything like that. And there's a great deal of interest in S&M in my books— it's also a political position. Let me put it politically: in a way, the hippie movement didn't work. It didn't work to say we're going to exert our power equally to yours, separately from yours. What seems to be working much more is a postmodernist or punk gesture which is much more about imitation, about guerrilla tactics, about reduplication, the whole situationist fad, and I'm very much interested in that.

Well, masochism is very deeply tied into that. Look at the power structures today; there's nothing you can do about the power structures, so politically you're in the position of the masochist. The masochist is powerless but has desires and somehow in the realm of the powerless has to act out desires. And that's a masochistic gesture, to turn against the self: "If you don't give me that money, I'm going to slit my wrists." A friend of mine did that in a punk club, and he got the money, where if he had said to this Mafia guy, "If you don't give me the money, I'm going to slit your wrists," he would've gotten killed. It's Gandhi's gesture, and it fascinates me.

It's also in personal relationships; in *Blood and Guts* that's the real kick, that Janey's actually taking pleasure in some way. If she were just a plain victim, that wouldn't have any power whatsoever. There are plenty of books that make the best seller lists, plain schlock, where the woman is pure victim. It's very typical of Anita Brookner.

I think some funny things are going on because the issues of power and self-control are so hot in feminist discourse. I think for women who are coming out of traditional training into marriage or whatever, it's very necessary to exert themselves and say, "I have power, I can do things." They don't want to see any other models of women; they can't deal with it, and maybe at that point they shouldn't. But I don't do that, I'm not in that position, I'm not in that world, and that's not my kind of writing. There are different kinds of writing, and not everybody's is for everybody's purpose.

Murphy: But many critics point to your characters as extremely powerless.

Acker: In *Tarantula* there is a woman pirate. And Janey, well, the publisher switched the chapters around, but in the end Janey dies and there are lots more Janeys over the earth. And I certainly don't see Don Quixote as powerless. I'm not showing a way out. I don't know one. If you know a way out, I'll listen.

The first time I ever had hints of it were with *Don Quixote*. And there are hints there for me. But that's the first time I ever had that. I don't think we know a way out. I don't think lesbian separatism is. I think we are trapped, not just women. I don't think my heroines are always women. It's a wandering through texts, that's what my books are and that's what I do. I see people as trapped, not only trapped politically, but by the very fact that they are a unit, have the limitations of consciousness, and a very miseducated consciousness.

Seriously, a lot of what has to be done now concerns what the new structures for freeing women's desire would look like, and very little work has been done about it. Mirrors of male activity are not going to work. At least one feminist view says that all men are evil and that women are totally good people and if they just establish a world with all their goodness, and get the evilness of men out there'll be paradise. That's simplifying that view, yet that's not simplifying it a lot, and it's really a mirror of the oppression by men. I think it's real dangerous for women who know they aren't like that, like the S&M lesbians; these women know they're not earth mothers and they're not totally good and that human sexuality doesn't look like that.

Murphy: When you talk about new structures tor women, what work do you see in that direction?

Acker: Oh, there are lots of discourses. Kristeva's work is important, so is Irigaray's in some weird way. Going outside that, I think there is going to be some Eastern, Arabic influence coming in, in its ways of seeing reality. We see so much divided into subject/object differences. It's all about centralization, the way we're taught to perceive. The centralization is in us, here, the perceiver, and there seems to be something basically wrong here. So I, subject, don't want to be object/victim; I want to be subject.

The Eastern way of seeing, that the object is the subject— if I'm talking to you now, then you're me, since you're my perception—makes a lot more sense and is probably a more workable model. Chinese, Japanese, whatever, Indian models, are probably more workable models.

Murphy: Or what's left of Haitian Voodoo.

Acker: Right, so back to talk of solutions. At the end of *Don Quixote* there's the hint of something, and it would be that, it would be based on models of perception, a sort of Third World meets semiotics. I just think we see things wrongly, it's why you would do so-called experimental writing, because the language doesn't work. It's all I/Other. But I don't know if there's going to be any way out, I don't know if we can anymore, at least not for humans.

Murphy: What issues do you try to bring out when you discuss pornography?

Acker: I don't think anyone knows what they are talking about when they talk about pornography. I don't think women who look anorexic in *Vogue* are any less pornographic than, say, women who are dominatrices in some porn novel. I mean, I'm more oppressed by anorexic women who walk around with no arms. I get to America, I turn on the hotel TV around noon, and the first thing I hear is, "Is there life after thirty? Can a woman find a husband?" Isn't that pornographic? I'd censor that before I would censor 42nd Street. I'd rather see Russ Meyer, that filmmaker who has all the women with big tits, than be told that I have no life because I'm over thirty.

Jay Murphy is a writer living in New York and editor of Red Bass.

12

Andres Serrano

Interviewed by Christian Walker

Andres Serrano's photo-based works have been the focus of controversy ever since his work Piss Christ *was singled out by Senator Jesse Helms and others in their attack on federal funding of the arts. Both before and since the controversy began, Serrano's work has often addressed issues of religion and the body, and he has recently also examined social and existential issues such as the Ku Klux Klan, homelessness, and the death of the human body. A distinctive aspect of his work is that even while addressing difficult social problems or bodily fluids (including menstrual blood, urine, and semen), the resulting photographs are formally beautiful. One of his works, depicting a Cardinal (portrayed by artist Leon Golub) beside a tortured, naked woman has often been reproduced in connection with articles and books on the censorship crises of the '90s, and this photograph encapsulates Serrano's ability to capture the underlying power that makes the nexus of sex, religion, and culture so problematic in the current era. Serrano has managed to use aesthetic means to focus difficult philosophical issues while simultaneously galvanizing the public around broad national issues of art and politics. The following interview took place in 1990.*

Christian Walker: Lucy Lippard has quoted you as saying your work derives from your unresolved feelings toward Catholicism. Can you talk about these feelings and how that is manifest in your work?

Andres Serrano: I'm drawn to the aesthetics of the Church and also to identify with Christ and what he stood for. But at the same time I don't like the direction the Church is heading in. Actually the Church has always been pretty oppressive, as far as dealing with women, blacks, minorities, gays, lesbians, and anyone else who doesn't go along with their program. So I'm drawn to Catholicism, or Christianity, but I have great difficulty with the Church itself.

Walker: I was an altar boy, and my cousin is a priest. That imagery shows up in my own work a lot.

Serrano: It's not a conscious decision on your part, I'm sure. It's something that is so inbred that you can't get away from it.

Walker: Your imagery also seems to be a stance of resistance to the culture as well as religion—a political resistance.

Serrano: I wouldn't define it too clearly (I don't mind if you do). But, yeah, there's this ambiguity in the work.

Walker: You'd see it as ambiguity as opposed to cultural resistance?

Serrano: Yeah, because I've never considered myself an activist, a champion of any sort in the social realm. I like to think in terms of raising more questions than answers.

Walker: What do you think about all the political references put on top of your work? There seems to be a strong political interpretation of your work both from the right and the left.

Serrano: I can't really fight that or complain about it because the work is meant to be open to interpretation, as I always say it is. I have to take it both ways, the good with the bad.

Walker: Do you see a political interpretation as bad?

Serrano: When the right uses the work to further their own agendas and completely distort what I'm trying to do, of course I see it as a gross misinterpretation of the work. But at the same time, I realize that perhaps part of the strength of the work is that it can be used that way, both ways. It's very satisfying as an artist when work can be accessible to more than just an art audience, can go from one arena to another.

Walker: Is that why you chose photography on some level, as being a more accessible medium?

Serrano: It certainly is more accessible for me and for my audience. I always think of myself as the artist and the audience, so that if it makes sense to me, if it strikes a chord in me, then I think and I hope that it will in others too.

Walker: Lippard has also said that your work is part of the polymorphous discourse that scholars have been calling for. Is multiculturalism a large theme for you?

Serrano: Not consciously, but I'm sure it's there, because I have a large multicultural aspect to me.

Walker: How much has your Afro-Caribbean background influenced your imagery? Did studying with Calvin Douglas, an African-American artist, influence your approach to artmaking?

Serrano: Specifically I can't say it has, but these influences operate on a variety of levels. My background is what you describe and then I also have European and Americanized influences. I would say that it mostly shows itself in the fact that I have a problem with, or I resist what I perceive as, homogenized white art. That is to say non-threatening work. I think for a person of color to do any work that is in some way threatening to a lot of people is indicative of where his roots are. The work of an artist like David Hammons doesn't have to be specifically black in order to be uncomfortable for a lot of people.

Walker: I see Hammons's work as being particularly Afrocentric, very much from the streets, very much from the culture of urbanized African-American people.

Serrano: I guess what I'm trying to say is that with some of his work, if you don't know the artist you don't necessarily think this is a black artist. You just know that it makes you uncomfortable but you don't quite know why.

Walker: Can you talk about your first run-in with censorship, with the stigmata piece? Did that affect the work that you made from that point?

Serrano: Lucy Lippard asked my wife (Julie Ault) and me to do a window at Printed Matter in 1984. We put two photographs in the window. Then someone on the block complained about the nude female figure with the stigmata. The figure next to it is a male nude who is carrying an animal carcass. She objected to the female figure. Lucy decided to turn the images around. We put a statement up saying why, and that was it. I did think about that. But the small incidents of censorship early on were insignificant. If the *Piss Christ* controversy hadn't taken place, I would never have given those instances a second thought. I had another piece called *Heaven or Hell* which showed a figure of a woman, naked from the waist up, hanging next to a man (Leon Golub) in a cardinal's suit. That piece was at a show at White Columns which at that time was in a Port Authority building and they got several complaints from several people who thought it was a Port Authority presentation. The gallery put up a disclaimer saying this was not a Port Authority presentation and had nothing to do with the Port Authority. That seemed to make people feel much better. Then there was another instance where a lab that printed my work, after they printed the stigmata picture, told me they couldn't print my work anymore.

Walker: *Heaven and Hell* deals with an image of a battered and bloody woman. Lippard talks about the overt sexuality and questions its possibly being a negative representation of women. How do you feel about the representation of women in your work, about the larger issues of eroticism in your work?

Serrano: I've not represented women a whole lot in my photographs, especially not from a sexual aspect. In that photograph I'm referring to the relationship the Church has with women, whether they are aware of women as human beings or just take them for granted and dismiss them. The cardinal in fact seems quite oblivious to the woman's suffering.

Walker: So you feel that's an image of a suffering woman, as opposed to an erotic image—even though the woman is voluptuous and her head is back. There is a strong erotic subtext to much of your work.

Serrano: I never thought of it as far as that picture was concerned. Then my friends would see it and say, "She has nice breasts." I never saw it that way. I've been looking at pornography since I was a kid, but to me that was not an erotic pose.

Walker: I think of my own work as anti-pornographic, although some of the work is an interracial interpretation of sexuality. Then someone said, "Oh, they're stag pictures," and that was a real shock to me. You really play off a lot of notions of masculinity and power, too.

Serrano: Sometimes it's hard to be politically correct and also be true to your own instincts, as far as sexuality is concerned.

Walker: In your new work you use semen and menstrual blood, which at some level has homoerotic connotations. A friend of mine mentioned that the "come shot" is a very homoerotic device. It moves sex from procreation to pleasure.

Serrano: The come shots for me are autoerotic as opposed to homoerotic. The only possible reference to homoeroticism I think is that in the age of AIDS, male sexuality is thought of in homosexual terms.

Walker: What do you think of using menstrual blood, in terms of its being a powerful feminist image of the '70s and '80s?

Serrano: I didn't think of it in terms of reclaiming that territory as a man, although Lippard kind of hinted at that. I thought of it more in terms of balancing the pictures about male sexuality and male reproduction with pictures about female reproduction, and bringing up the question of female reproduction rights. A lot of people have more problems with those pictures than they do with the come shots, which are very aestheticized, beautiful, unthreatening to them. In a way they're also horizontal and passive. The other pictures are vertical and much more aggressive, and question the whole notion of masculine and feminine. It makes people feel uncomfortable sometimes because of the whole notion of wanting to look at women and not wanting to look at women, not wanting to take them seriously enough.

Walker: So there is a certain feminist analysis?

Serrano: A little bit. I would never claim to be politically correct, but I'm learning. Over the years, my wife and women friends have taught me that I have a lot to learn about male-female relationships.

Walker: Does your wife have a large influence on your work? Do you still collaborate with her?

Serrano: She's been my biggest supporter. We don't really collaborate. I'll show her a photograph or tell her an idea and she'll give me the nod or no. Now she gives me a lot more nods than she used to.

Walker: The whole notion of body fluids in your work seems to be about the age of AIDS, but also about the primitive, alchemy, and healing and ritual ceremony.

Serrano: All that stuff is traditionally more important to the non-white artist than the white artist. I try to personalize the work, and that's why I draw on these things. My work is not terribly intellectual or theoretical. I want it to be accessible, to be personal, and at the same time I hope it strikes a universal chord.

Walker: But it's very, very intelligent work, too. There's a large intellectual component.

Serrano: I'm not one of those artists concerned with theory and strategy.

Walker: But it's all there in the work. Your work was the most intriguing work in the "Ten Hispanic Photographers" show. Most of the work was fairly transparent. I thought that your work in the show was not particularly Hispanic: you were dealing with more universal things, with primitivism, with Africanism, religion—things that are important to minorities in the larger culture.

Serrano: If I have anything to be proud of as an artist, it's the fact that I am a Hispanic person who's not thought of as a Hispanic artist, necessarily. I've been in very few Hispanic shows, and I don't mind being in them, and I don't mind not being in them. I think it's important for artists of color to be aware that there's a tendency, if you let society do it to you, to segregate you and ghettoize you. It's important not to be lost in the shuffle.

Walker: Benny Andrews talks about that in terms of his own work. If you're a black artist in America you get called every February, Black History Month, to exhibit. There seems to be some influence in your work from the West African influence on Catholicism.

Serrano: Catholicism in this country means one thing and in Europe it means another thing and in Latin America and the Caribbean it means something else—and it's still Catholicism. Catholicism takes many forms and has many colors.

Walker: Your work also fits in the whole discourse of postmodernism, the discussion of media and representation, your references to Western art and classical European art. How much is your work influenced by all that?

Serrano: I don't take part in those discussions but I'm glad to be part of the discourse.

Walker: How has Western art influenced your work? There seems to be a tension between abstraction and narrative in your work, for example.

Serrano: Marcel Duchamp influenced me as he did the whole world. Abstraction has influenced me, and people like Luis Buñuel. The dada and surrealist idea of juxtaposing the strange with the normal, the mundane with the monumental.

Walker: There is also an element of classical composition in your work.

Serrano: I think composition is very important. In art school I started in painting and sculpture and that gave me a feel for composition. You have to be able to successfully translate an idea in a visually effective manner, so you have to have exciting composition.

Walker: Your work is very internal, it's not at all in the documentary tradition of photography.

Serrano: My early work was street portraits. But sometime around '83 I decided I wanted to become a tableau photographer. I wanted to take the pictures in my head rather than pictures that I found out there.

Walker: What photographers were you inspired by?

Serrano: One of my all time favorite photographers has been Julia Margaret Cameron. I think her portraits are extremely strong. Some people saw her as an amateur; she didn't have the right equipment, her pictures weren't crystal clear. But as far as I'm concerned, she took some of the best photographs ever taken. The reason I feel an affinity with her is that as a photographer, I'm not that interested in the technical aspects of photography. For years I used the same lights and camera and I never learned to print. I think I'm more an artist with a camera than a real photographer. I would say that sometimes I'm anti-photography.

Walker: Cameron's work deals with allegory and the transcendental state and mysticism. All of which your work deals with.

Serrano: But some of the portraits are so direct, that you get beyond all that and you just see them as beautiful portraits. Another person I've always liked is Edward Curtis. I never realized that Curtis was controversial...

Walker: For his portrayal of Native Americans. How did you manage to stay out of that political discourse on someone who made work that was so charged?

Serrano: I guess mostly by concentrating on the work. I've just completed a new series that refers to the portraits he did of American Indians. I went around with a friend who helped me carry my equipment, including a photographic background, a battery operated lighting system, an umbrella, a tripod. I went around and found homeless people in the subways, in the street, in the parks. I even found people looking through garbage. I was looking for the hard core homeless that sometimes even the homeless don't want to talk to. We set them up in subways in situations and took their portraits, studio portraits. I was not in a position to take the homeless to a studio so I took the studio to the homeless. Basically, I gave them a fee to pose for me for fifteen minutes, and had them sign model releases.

When the whole *Piss Christ* controversy erupted, I said that I didn't have a problem with disturbing work, provocative work. I said that in fact I looked forward to the day when I could take pictures that were disturbing to me. That's why I took these pictures, to explore the nature of that discomfort, to be able to look at that fine line we walk between exploration and exploitation.

Walker: When you start doing work like that people confuse it with documentary. Avedon ran into that with his pictures of the West.

Serrano: Curtis's portraits are documentation, but I also think that they're more than documentation.

Walker: They have a romantic, Westernized notion of Native Americans.

Serrano: Right. Which I find refreshing, compared to Hollywood's version of events and portrayal of American Indians. Basically those are the only two reference points I have for American Indians—Westerns that I grew up with in the '50s and '60s, and the pictures of Curtis.

Walker: How do you see the new pictures of yours fitting into that?

Serrano: I see these pictures as being also about marginality and invisibility. On a personal level it was very satisfying to relate to people one to one that I would never have looked at under different circumstances. People who are sometimes quite abnormal by our standards, except that for fifteen or twenty minutes we had a traditional photographer-model relationship. I took pictures of one woman who I'm sure was a crackhead. She had problems focusing her eyes. Her head and eyes darted very quickly. But she's one of my favorite portraits. She's beautiful.

Walker: That brings up contradictions, like the idea that the work could be romanticized because it becomes very beautiful.

Serrano: That's the whole point. Why should the homeless be looked at only in a certain way. I think you're talking about a certain prejudice if we think these pictures are bad because the homeless aren't being portrayed like they really are. What does that mean? These pictures are more collaborations with the subjects than documentations or fictionalizations. Who says the homeless can't have studio portraits like everyone else?

Walker: Your picture *Dread* seems to have some of that kind of energy. To me that seems like a picture of resistance; it makes me think of Public Enemy's album *Fear of a Black Planet*. It seems like one of your most political images.

Serrano: I guess it would be. I've always identified with the music of the streets, specifically hip-hop. As far as I'm concerned it's better to have anarchy in the clubs than real revolution in the streets. I don't see why people feel so threatened by the music. Maybe they don't want to remember that at one time young people were more militant than they are now. They weren't just making music, they were planning revolutions.

Walker: And soon will be again.

Serrano: If the trend continues.

Walker: You have a series called "The Blacks"; could you talk about them?

Serrano: It was an unsuccessful series for me, but it was a necessary step for me. It led me to the "nomads" pictures which is what the Curtis-inspired work is about.

Walker: What were you going after when you were doing the series, why was it unsuccessful for you?

Serrano: It was difficult for me to do technically; I didn't have the right lighting equipment. Maybe I'll redo it, but I've kind of lost interest. But there were a couple of shots that were very good.

Walker: I was interested in the reference to the Genet work, that sets up a supreme white culture and a black culture that imitates it and, in control, becomes the white culture. It's an unbelievably pessimistic view of revolution, change, or progression. It mirrors the '80s, the emergence of minorities, but the class structure is getting much more divided, or much poorer.

Serrano: And angrier on both sides.

Walker: What I found interesting about the controversy is Scott Tyler is a black man, you're identified as a Hispanic artist, Mapplethorpe is a gay artist. There seemed to be a notion that Third World people and people who were outside mainstream culture are also activist. I question that if the terms were different, if it had been a white male heterosexual artist doing the work (although he wouldn't have been doing work like this anyway), it would have been different. How do you feel about your work being resistant to culture?

Serrano: I think I'm in good company with those guys.

Christian Walker is an artist and critic best known for manipulated photographs exploring racial and personal histories.

13

Karen Finley

Interviewed by Nicholas Drake

Karen Finley was already well known as a performance artist when she was denied a National Endowment for the Arts grant in 1990 (along with Tim Miller, Holly Hughes, and John Fleck) by the National Council for the Arts, after the peer review panel had awarded grants to each of the artists. The resulting case of the NEA 4 was a cause célèbre in the arts community and a touchstone in the right-wing attacks on art and arts funding. The case was ultimately settled out of court, but the NEA has continued to override panel awards, recently in the case of an award to Andres Serrano unanimously approved by the panel and then canceled by the National Council. Finley's work has often dealt with the body, child abuse, violence, and oppression, often through performances marked by a trance-like stage presence and nudity. Her work attacks the limited moral scope and vindictive reactionary character of the dominant social forms prevalent in the United States today. She is not, however, advocating an anarchistic or utopian removal of all social constraints, as is clear in the following interview. She is instead conducting a profoundly critical, personal, and moral analysis of contemporary human relations. The provocations that she sets in motion in her works are so effective in galvanizing the cultural cleansers at large in our society because those forces recognize the critical power and moral force that she embodies in her work. She has also published several books, including Shock Treatment, *a collection of texts drawn from her performance work, and* Enough is Enough, *a comic self-help manual. Her performance work* A Certain Level of Denial *was touring the U.S. in 1994, when this interview was conducted.*

Nicholas Drake: Where did your career start?

Karen Finley: I went to the Chicago Art Institute, and then to the San Francisco Art Institute.

Drake: You studied visual art?

Finley: I've always considered performance art to be a visual art. I've always done painting and other forms.

Drake: So along with drawing and painting, you've been performing the whole time?

Finley: I've been doing some type of conceptual work since puberty. I was aware of Happenings and things like that. It was just natural. I did action/Happening things with groups of people in school, and later I did performance with other artists I had met. It just naturally evolved that I was doing more performance when I was in San Francisco. It was never a deviation, it was a natural progression. I'm originally from Evanston, Illinois, a very progressive town. I was doing conceptual-based work very early on because I went to the Chicago Art Institute, where they had performance, in grade school and high school, and in my high school, performance went along with regular art making.

I was always interested in drawing, and figure drawing. I've always been interested in the body and in communicating with people. I would do things like sit and write next to people on the bus. I would write to strangers. With most people, performance and conceptual work is something that comes about when they're in college, or when they have been painting for a long time. But I look at my work—which most people think is very controversial—as being in a tradition. I was doing performance work and involved in conceptually based concepts when I was twelve and thirteen years old. I came from a very progressive educational background. I think that that is important because it shows the reason why I am very comfortable in the kind of work that I do. Though people may look at what I do—taking off my clothes and so forth—as shocking, I never have looked at any of my work or ideas as shocking. I've looked at it as part of a tradition of conceptual and body artists. I thought that I was just part of that tradition. And my parents were very supportive towards my work, as was my community, to the point that choosing art for a career was looked at in the same way as someone going into the sciences. I think that's important, because I feel comfortable, and I think that has helped me a lot in my career.

Drake: When you moved out of that kind of environment, did you realize that people took what you were doing as shocking or revolutionary?

Finley: I didn't find that until my grant from the NEA, when I was brought into the media. Getting a master's degree and going through that system of being with my peers, I saw myself as a professional. What was very difficult or devastating for me in the NEA experience was being looked at as if I were crazy, out of control, or unprofessional. That's what I hate the most about the way artists are perceived by most of American culture. They are looked at as if they're crazy or don't have any sense of morals, or don't have any sense of responsibility, and that basically they are also thieves, that they are just out to get the most out of things. I found that very difficult.

My reaction was depression. It hurt me so much because I felt that that was my identity. But first I had my public responsibility, which was suing the government, the NEA. Any other artist could have been in my place, too, so I felt that public responsibility. But in my private life, it was very difficult. I was hearing things like, "Oh, aren't you lucky that this is happening to you!" I never wanted to exploit this situation at all, to make a career move out of it. In fact, I turned down anything that had to do with the NEA, which created problems with some of the other plaintiffs. I just could not handle being in the position of having to constantly defend my work.

Drake: So, you were battling for your integrity.

Finley: I felt that it was my public and moral responsibility to sue the government, and to try to be as professional as possible. Maintaining a certain professionalism, a certain standard, was always very important to me. When lies were made up about me in the media constantly, it was difficult, because I am a very private person.

Drake: You had to fight a certain image that was growing up around you, that didn't accurately represent your work.

Finley: Correct. I think many times women just have that. If I take my shirt off, immediately I am sexualized, whereas if a man takes off his, he's going to work. A woman immediately generates so much fear as soon as she shows her feelings or is strong. Just the words that are used—it was always that I was hysterical or that there was an out of control eroticism or unbridled sexuality, like I was some animal. And the chocolate...they just totally reversed all that my work is about. I became what I was talking about. I wondered many times, "What am I doing this for?" A lot of my work is somehow a Rorschach test; it brings up different things for different people. People have certain issues that they are dealing with, and they project them onto me. So it really isn't about my art, it's that I'm bringing something up that isn't necessarily talked about. I don't spend a lot of time analyzing the reactions to my work. Many times people who have a strong reaction to my work haven't necessarily even seen it.

There are lots of different looks to my work, too. My visual work can sometimes be very symbolic or lyrical. I like to display paintings so that you look at them and the symbolism grows on you. It isn't something that you get in three seconds. I like work that is more time based. There are a lot of different sides of me in my work. Some work is mournful, some is angry, some is funny. What runs through all my work is intensity. What I do is the feeling—I always try to genuinely react very honestly. That's what makes my performance different than in theater— I have text and then I'm responding to that text in a genuine manner rather than acting towards it.

Drake: Some of the imagery in your performance—for example the little rocking horse and the way you used the rocking motion with the horse's detached head—has an almost nonrational quality to it, above and beyond reason. It has an intuitive character that is very evocative. I was very struck by the kind of imagery you used, like the series of gray and black projections in the background and the way you throw your shadow across them. I don't think that anything that I've heard or read about you talks about the strength of your visual imagery.

Finley: Visuals are very important to me. There was an article in *High Performance* by Jacki Apple, and, although she says something cynical about me that she doesn't get right, I do have to agree with her that performance art has kind of lost the idea, that people don't realize it's a visual art form. Many monologists and standup comics are calling themselves performance artists.

I use my body as a prop and a visual element, and I use a set as an installation. *A Certain Level of Denial* is supposed to be more like a dream or cinema, which is why there are things that aren't completely rational—like the rocking horse. I wanted the shadow to be more raw, so the lighting is mostly done by a slide projector.

I start from visuals. I do the paintings first, and then the story; then I arrange and write the text, and somehow they're always connected. I've always worked more from a visual source, as opposed to an artist like Eric Bogosian, who studies characters. He comes more from a theater background. I don't put as much attention toward my character studies—I don't really do characters—as I do the visuals. In fact, there are many places where I cannot perform because I have to set up the installation.

Drake: You go into a trance-like state. How do you approach that trance?

Finley: It's different from an acting state. It's going with the emotion; it's a very deep concentrated state, but I can feel and know what's going on in the rest of the room. In some performance pieces, like *We Keep Our Victims Ready*, I read some of the text, and in *A Certain Level of Denial* you see me reading sometimes—I go out of and come back to the trance.

In the beginning, when I'm talking to the audience, I'm preparing myself, too, centering myself. For me a good performance is emotionally very genuine, there is some kind of contact or connection or breakthrough made. That happens at different times in the work.

Drake: When did you first use that trance-state?

Finley: Well, I worked as a psychic. I've always had ways to kind of go into deep concentrated states. I think if you're working on something, whether it's writing, or art, it's a deep concentrated space. You're just there, or not even necessarily there.

Drake: What about the more textual, more intellectual and conceptual part of your work?

Finley: My work is a reaction to my becoming aware, in my early twenties, that there weren't really many women artists. I had the sense that my body and emotions were in the way. At that point, I made a conscious decision to exploit the feminine limitations that were given to me, and hang them over the audience's heads, the *male* audience in particular. I was told that my body and my gender would keep me from being an artist, and I have always been interested in looking into these areas.

I came into performance when there were artists like Sol LeWitt and Carl Andre minimalizing everything—I went to the opposite, I maximized everything, or at least gave emotions to respond to.

At that point in performance, there weren't many artists using politics or child abuse or disorder. It was more about abstraction—I don't mean this in a mean way, but men had the privilege of making work about size or paint or length or duration or even abstraction. I started with what I felt, freeing me from what I had been imprisoned by, by exposing my gender's limitations.

Drake: You use yourself, your body as a canvas or an art medium.

Finley: Well, I think we all use ourselves that way. I want to show that, and I think that by coming out nude I do. Also because, coming from a visual arts background and the tradition of figure drawing, I like the figure. I also think it's funny, because there is so much expectation when a woman gets undressed, but it's very unsexy if the woman comes out nude. In burlesque, the woman starts out dressed and takes her clothes off, because the audience wants to see her. If I come out nude in the beginning, it takes the whole game away.

Drake: Little by little throughout a piece, you put on more and more clothing, until at the end, you have actually dressed yourself.

Finley: Yes, I actually think it's funny. I'm showing the ridiculousness of some of these objects that we adorn ourselves with, like stockings and gloves. I come out with the shoes and the hat, which are really kind of ridiculous animal-like articles that we adorn ourselves with. Like a feathered hat, or "mules," as they call pumps. And the gloves, which are like claws. Or stockings—when you look at them they are kind of a weird idea. It can be comical. I don't think there's a lot of humor within sexuality, really. We have a problem with combining humor and sexuality.

I also like the idea that my body is getting older. I just had a baby, and because I have been breast feeding, I have a different kind of body. My breasts are a different shape. I have some fat to keep my milk supply going. I have a different type of a body than a classic nude. I actually like it better now that I have more of a woman's body than I did when I was in my early twenties.

Drake: What do you think about censorship in general, and do you push your expression against certain mores, taboos, and limitations?

Finley: Censorship is devastating, and I think that in America we are seeing a chilling effect. I don't receive any public funding. I also feel that there are different ways of censoring. There is art censorship. There is class censorship (if you are poor you have a lot less access). You can be censored just by your gender, your sex, too.

I've never really felt that I pushed a button. I feel that I am following in a tradition of art, including Chris Burden, Vito Acconci, and so forth. I don't go into my studio and say, "Hey, how can I rock someone's boat?" In fact, I always thought that some of my work was tame. I thought to myself that people were going to think that it was stupid. Not that I really even care. I would just do it anyway.

Drake: How do you see your work evolving?

Finley: What I do now is mostly installation work. I would like to be able to go more mainstream. It's just that the mainstream doesn't want to go with me. I'd like to have a TV show. I'd love to have access to movies. I wish that artists or art could become more mainstream without losing its edge, that you didn't have to compromise. I wish that becoming mainstream didn't mean that you have to lose any of your integrity. I would like to be able to reach as many people as possible.

Nicholas Drake *is an artist and writer who lives in Charleston, South Carolina.*

14

Yvonne Rainer

Interviewed By David Laderman

Yvonne Rainer began her artistic career as a dancer and choreographer in New York City in the '60s. In the early '70s, she switched to film. Her works include: Lives of Performers, Film About a Woman Who..., Kristina Talking Pictures, Journeys from Berlin/1971, The Man Who Envied Women, *and, since this 1989 interview was conducted,* Privilege *and* MURDER *and murder. Her early films incorporate a very "choreographic" sensibility: gesture, posture, posing, and body movement are treated as deliberate exercises in visual and emotional expression, producing a striking tableau effect. Yet working in conjunction with this gestural aesthetic is a remarkable sense of cinematic innovation. While all her films can be loosely characterized as fictional, they often mobilize meta-fictional discourses and intratextual tensions: she uses voice-overs, at times confessional, at times analytic, to comment upon the image track; the camera movements and angles are daringly self-conscious; subtitles and intertitles provide counterpoint to the images and voice-overs. Her films perpetually interrogate and reformulate traditional cinematic narrative. Character identification is undermined by various means, and narrative closure is foregone in favor of ambiguous layers of unresolved queries.*

Such tactics are not merely formal devices in Rainer's work; rather, they serve to explore emotional crisis, alienation, and seduction, in works that are both critiques of and alternatives to the dominant stereotypes of women. While she continues to examine the interpersonal dramas of romance and seduction, she has in her more recent works explicitly addressed social and political realities, including the problems of minority and artist housing in New York, U.S. sponsored violence in Central America, and the experience of aging for women in American society. The following discussion raises issues of radical thought on both aesthetic and social planes.

David Laderman: Does your work as a filmmaker evolve from your earlier work as a dancer and choreographer?

Yvonne Rainer: I can talk about my evolution from dance to film on two fronts. One has to do with content, the other has to do with form. The content of my early films came as a response to the second coming of feminism, which gave me permission to explore my experience as a woman, as a female subject. Although the form of these films had been influenced by Warhol and Hollis Frampton, their emotional, "female" subject matter suggested women's weepies and soap opera.

Laderman: There has been a lot written about melodrama recently—your first film was subtitled "a melodrama." A lot of people see melodrama as a marginalized site in Hollywood where woman's desire is articulated. How do you see your relationship to melodrama: are you trying to rework it?

Rainer: I never came to these things from a theoretical perspective. I didn't set out to rework melodrama, although in a way you might say the films do. I was aware of certain aspects of melodrama. For instance, in *Film About a Woman Who...*, the thunder that keeps coming up to suggest dire events. There was often an irony going, similar to the ways in which I used classical and baroque music in my dancing to invoke a sense of grandeur, or tragedy, or destiny, in contrast to very slight or unportentous physical effort.

Laderman: Why would you want to invoke that grandeur?

Rainer: I was interested in certain conventions and traditions and certain kinds of inflations that were no longer appropriate, and I was interested in ordinary movement, the nonspectacle of people just jogging around the space, for instance. I would accompany that with organ music of Buxtehude, which would be undercut by what you were actually seeing. It was a way of using the minimalist vernacular, as far as movement went, and invoking two traditions, a modernist one and a traditional one, having one's cake and eating it. Of course the end effect was irony, which was its limitation or maybe its inevitability. There is still that aspect to my work. In those early films, the expression of the most dire events, like emotional dissolution, rage, the

Sturm und Drang of sexual conflict is always expressed in a very matter-of-fact, ordinary way. And in the way it's presented it eludes the conventions of enactment of cinematic narrative. With that kind of undercutting by stating something so baldly and directly, I think the end result is a clue to an attitude that this is to be taken as a very contrived kind of representation, and you're not to get too involved in this.

Laderman: Related to that, in a lot of your films, I've noticed a strong interest in spectators and watching.

Rainer: The act of looking is foregrounded as well as a kind of self-consciousness about exposure and about the confessional mode which suggests autobiography and exorcism or catharsis. The irony and the displacements and the incongruities are a kind of distanciation effect.

Laderman: Since we started talking about melodrama and Hollywood, of the films you've seen in popular cinema, do you feel that the feminist movement has had an impact on popular films?

Rainer: There are all kinds of new female heroines, but very often the same kinds of closures persist. The woman gets punished in some way or gets married. In *Fatal Attraction* a woman's overweening desire is punished. Or in *Working Girl*, there are two women who are independent career women, but they're doing the same old thing, fighting over a man, and the woman who is most liberated of course is punished. Sigourney Weaver is the villain because she is the boss, so she has to be shot down. Women in authority are still a very threatening proposition. But these films have the earmarks of feminist liberation. Men's pulling of the strings is now more complicated.

Laderman: Of the five films you've made between 1972 and 1985, how would you describe your evolution as a filmmaker?

Rainer: There is an ongoing thread, a continuity in terms of the relation of the individual, of private life, to public life, an emerging political consciousness on different fronts. That began in a rather naive way with *Kristina Talking Pictures*, the third film. By *Journeys from Berlin* I was dealing with specific historical events, the Baader Meinhof activity and political violence, contrasting three cultures, the North American psychoanalytic culture versus the political activism in which Russian nihilist women's actions are compared to those of the Baader Meinhof group. Then getting closer to home with the last film, housing, U.S. involvement in Central America. These things are looked at from a fictionalized private life, a disrupted marriage, with a woman observing the activities of her husband while she's dealing with her own social urgencies. I guess my interests have proliferated around the subjectivity of emotional life in relation to specific social/political arenas.

Laderman: A lot of feminist critics have written about your films—do you see yourself as a feminist film maker? In the context of the neoconservative climate in which there is a hesitancy to align oneself with feminism, a lot of artists don't want to take that militant position. Do you see feminism still as a viable, powerful force?

Rainer: It's absolutely necessary. I think sexism and racism are the two areas or dynamics that continue to affect people's lives in the most destructive ways, and they are both parallel and different and have to be continually examined and reassessed and articulated as sites for social change. I don't think the women's movement is done with or has been allowed to accomplish a fraction of what it should accomplish. My own area of concern has shifted or broadened: I'm dealing with aging, which, for a woman, very much has to do with attitudes about sexuality. My interests keep up with my own life processes. There's always a new rock to overturn to see what's underneath.

Laderman: I'm interested in your use of nonsynchronous sound, with different voice-overs ambiguously located in the film text, commenting on the images or digressing from them, perhaps bringing together traditionally disparate areas. Kaja Silverman describes this as a feminist strategy in that it deconstructs the homocentric Cartesian subjectivity that keeps body and voice together so that the male can discursively and in a specular way dominate the female. How do you conceive this technique as a feminist approach?

Rainer: I do not have a programmatic theory for this kind of strategy. It belongs to a modernist sense of representing the world. The centrality of the colonialist male voice has to be toppled. It's a matter of choice for the artist to either go with that as a general principle or to recenter another kind of subjectivity. I think I've done both. In *The Man Who Envied Women*, there is a female centrality. I have displaced her physically, I have refused to provide an image that risks a potential for traditional sexual objectification. I have decentered her physicality, while recentering her as a voice, as a presence, as a subjectivity, as a spectator, as one who looks, as an observer-commentator. I don't think there necessarily has to be a relationship between that decentering of the voice and a feminist project. I don't think that it is as a feminist that I choose these strategies, it is as an artist who has developed in a certain way at a certain time. I'm very interested in seeing these subjectivities re-centered that have not had a chance to be centered, that have always been on the margin. These are black people and other people of color. More and more Asians and blacks and Third World people are insisting on the centering of their own experience, and this is rightfully so. It's interesting that recently there seems to be this conflation of, or association of, avant-garde strategies with the white imperialist position. This is perceived as part of the history of Eurocentric art. But it's also a continuing, viable language. I disagree with this notion that certain feminists have put forth that language is by definition and in essence male. Language is all we've got and it's available to be used. It can be used in different ways. I think it's the same with these distanciating, Brechtian, decentering strategies. They're available to be used in different ways. The language of the avant-garde can be a progressive force or can be as exclusionary as any other. It would be interesting to look at avant-garde film tradition and uncover its oppressive biases: it's already been done in the area of sexuality. But I doubt if such a critical project would necessarily discredit non-narrative strategies in and of themselves. And, of course, the massive absence of race as an issue or generative force in film until recently is itself a damning critique.

Laderman: Are you saying that the language of the avant-garde is available to be used for more politically...

Rainer: ...liberating projects, yes. It is not in and of itself progressive, or radical simply because it topples a previous aesthetic position.

Laderman: Because it can be reactionary, as we've seen in a self-enclosed, and isolated and elitist project.

Rainer: Not only elitist, but promoting transcendental subjectivities that belong to the dominant sex or race or class.

Laderman: Teresa de Lauretis, in *Technologies of Gender*, suggests that you were addressing a gendered spectator in *The Man Who Envied Women*, a woman spectator, and she describes this as a feminist strategy.

Rainer: I didn't know how much this was so at the time. I knew the primary subjectivity was that of a woman, but to my surprise, the male character has been pretty consistently vilified, judging from people's responses. I had thought he would be a more sympathetic character. I was trying to create a complex person, but most people find him pretty negative. I think that's a matter of direction, of tone. I keep discovering this, that there are subtleties of voice and intonation that carry more weight than I had given them credit for. I recently came in upon a screening at a crucial moment, and I had a response to the voice-over of Jack Deller, the main character, "Oh my god, this sounds supercilious." This is a point when the guy is supposed to express passionate conviction about what he is saying, and there is something a little bit cynical about his voice, and I had never heard that before. I still have a lot to learn as a director. You have to be more and more sensitized to these nuances.

Laderman: I felt I could identify with him, but it was in ways I didn't like.

Rainer: That was always part of my intention, but only part.

Laderman: De Lauretis also talks about your use of narrative in the film, and she seems to be defending the use of narrative. Yet she quotes you from an article you wrote about your suspicion in your drift towards narrative. Were you trying to use narrative to interrogate it?

Rainer: It's always a dual project. I agree with Teresa in a lot of ways in her critique of narrative, not just that it's an Oedipal enterprise, but in the way it is carried out by cinematic conventions and traditions, it does carry oppressive ideologies. In the way it's used in mass culture, it reconfirms social roles and it always has that possibility. Which is not to say that by contravening narrative or undermining it you necessarily contravene these positions. But you do sidestep, and my relation to it is a continual flirtation and side stepping, not foxtrotting, but sidestepping. You do have to give people things they recognize. In seeing *Film About a Woman Who...* again last night I realized that there is so little that is recognizable in the images of the people. They are like Martians. There is a lot that's recognizable in the language, but the people are so tightly controlled and choreographed that they are ciphers. I guess that was very deliberate at the time. I wanted all of the emotional impact to come through in voice-over and titles. That was partly a delusion on my part, but at that point I really wanted to create the same catharses and Aristotelian effects that classical drama and cinema had. And I thought I was going to revolutionize film, but then I discovered it was a much more complicated matter than I had thought. It still terrifies me to be giving over a project to actors and to those insidious skills of theirs. I still see the totally realized illusionistic project as running aground, being shipwrecked. I agree very much with Alexander Kluge when he talks about opera, in the same way that I think about narrative. He gives people little pieces of opera or narrative, enough for people to be seduced, and recognize themselves in a romantic or illusionist space or in what passes for social spaces, whether it be in love or in public life. Like little pieces of story, interaction, shot reverse shot, music, it makes for a kind of cultural comfort. I think people do need this kind of support, relief. But then on the back of that, using those conventions as a kind of armature, as a departure for more difficult, demanding representations, be it theoretical material, the excessive gab that I like to get into, or these extreme discrepancies between sound and image. And

formal and intellectual and political things that are not so root-
ed in these recognizable formulations.

Laderman: There have been a lot of books published recently
about men in feminism. In the first chapter of De Lauretis's
Technologies of Gender she criticizes some male theorists for
taking up the metaphor of woman in an appropriating way. You
seem to be making the same criticism, in your last film's treatment of Jack as a "new man" or your critique of the "About Men"
column, which I found extremely incisive. As a man who would
like to participate in the feminist struggle in some sort of con-
structive way, I'm interested in what kind of role you see men
playing in the feminist struggle in general or perhaps even in
how they can be represented in films.

Rainer: I think I'm facing the same problem in dealing with
issues of racism, as a white middle class avatar, you might say,
of cultural supremacy. You have to acknowledge your position of
advantage, certainly. You can't, as Trinh Minh-ha says, speak
for the other. You have to speak beside the other. And this is
certainly a case where you have to have the voice of the other
there, and it's a very tricky balance, but you don't want a balancing act. After three years of struggling with a new script, I
realize that it's a matter of foreground and background. Even
where you have the voice of the (female or non-white) "other"—
from the point of view of a man, a woman's voice, from my point
of view, a black voice—that voice can still be coopted or undermined by the position of the author, who in my case is a white
woman. At this point I see it as partly a topological problem.
What ends up being the predominant or uppermost voice? It
very much has to do with the terrain that's being covered. I
know in my case in this new film even though it starts out being
a story by (for, to) a white woman, it has to end up foreground-
ing the subjectivity of a black woman, and that's what I'm trying
to do. I think men have something to contribute to feminism
other than lending support to women's efforts. I would be interested in men talking about their sexism. But it's tricky: does it
end up being "poor me" or "us victims"? "About Men" should be
more about sexism. The column now appears every other week
in the Sunday *Times* Magazine, alternating with "Hers," so now

they share equal time. But even the women's column is mostly about experiences of motherhood and their own mothers, and sexism is rarely the issue. Men most often talk about their sons or their fathers. There was one, however, that fascinated me, about a man who went on a deep sea diving trip. When he was on the bottom he got a signal that he must come up immediately, because something was wrong with the generator on the deck, and he had very little air left. Later, when he realized how close a call he'd had, he felt the most extreme contempt for his wife and children and his role as a father and husband. He couldn't understand it. Somehow the exhilaration of that brush with oblivion made him feel total contempt for his life as a man with obligations to women and children (that's the way I interpret it; he didn't put it that way). I thought that was an amazing confession and explains a lot about men's projects in the world, from war to various kinds of aggrandizement, going to sea, going into space—a flight from women, even at the cost of their lives. He had no idea or theory about what had happened. When he told the story to friends, they said, "Oh, it was just an emotional reaction." The event was left totally up in the air. It was one of the most interesting and suggestive revelations in that column. Men's contributions to feminism might be anecdotes or analyses of experiences like that.

Laderman: I sense that patriarchy is rebounding from feminism and appropriating it and twisting it.

Rainer: In academia.

Laderman: And in mass culture, like in the films we were talking about earlier. With this idea of the "new man," the men are benefiting, but the women are not, really.

Rainer: Family life may be changing, but it's still the woman who has the earliest and most consistent physical contact with a child. I wonder if that's changing, or do both parents have less and less contact because both have to work? I don't know if these changes in family life have an effect on male supremacy. People like Dorothy Dinnerstein (*The Mermaid and the Minotaur*) have pointed to the early handling of the infant for its profound effect on gender relations.

Laderman: Many male theorists use the notion of the femi-nine in their theories but they don't address these issues of their own sexism. In *The Man Who Envied Women* you've obviously given a lot of thought to the wave of theory that's overtaking humanities departments in the U.S. I was especially fascinated with the way you filmed the lecture sequence with Jack. He's going on and on, spinning this vast web of Foucault and Lacan and yet the camera's gliding around in a slow arc and you can hear some of the directorial comments. You're filming the zom-bie students, then the camera wanders around the rest of the loft. I felt I could identify with the way you were representing this dissemination of theory. What I caught, coming from my position as a student of this theory, is that this is just jargon, it's dead, it's having no effect, it's a pure artifice. How do you see this whole wave of theory that's informing all these men in these departments?

Rainer: There's always theory, you rub two ideas together and you've got theory. I'm dealing not so much with the theory itself as with a certain use of it. There are two sequences that spew out theory in that film. The hallway sequence deals with the eroticization of theory. That is something that has struck me, that certain kinds of discourse have the potential for erotic aggrandizement and seduction, which isn't played out in the classroom but can be played out in a one-to-one situation. The other sequence is partly about the power professors have over students. I missed the boat a little bit with the lecture sequence. The real estate value of that space should have been foreground-ed much earlier. If I were to do it again I would put a big banner on the wall, with a Helmsley-Spear slogan, "Move up to down-town" or something gentrifying like that. The idea is that a loft space—a prime piece of NY real estate—has been put on the market, and that leads in to the disappeared in urban centers and then the disappeared in Central America. The assault on the poor. I wasn't commenting on his lecture; I didn't want you to feel you had to follow what he was saying that closely. You cannot follow it, it's full of digressions. It's like a six-month sur-vey course crammed into twelve minutes. It is frustrating; he speeds up. I played around with the sound, overriding it with the crew talking, but the real estate theme should have been more clear. I could have done it differently by starting in the kitchen, establishing the space.

Laderman: E. Ann Kaplan has a new anthology called *Postmodernism and its Discontents*. The title itself indicates a pervasive problem with the term "postmodernism." I wonder if you find the term useful to characterize your work?

Rainer: It's confusing, it's a way of marking off, for territorial reasons, new areas for critics to operate in. I think it's a new sphere of consumption. I don't think it operates to illuminate anything. I think poststructuralism is more apt, to indicate changes since Levi-Strauss and the use of semiotics. "Postmodernism" is like "pluralism." I have a personal reason for disapproving of the term. I was trained in modern dance, a term that was absolutely clear in its meaning: "not ballet." As early as 1963, to differentiate what the Judson group did from previous modern dance, pre-Cunningham, I used the term post-modern, a very specific use. Again it was territorial, to carve out a niche. It's a career move, and it suggests a break with the past, when really these kinds of breaks are at best arbitrary. At worst confusing.

Laderman: I find your films very political, in their critique of representation and ideology. Do you see any kind of future for a political avant-garde?

Rainer: Constantly.

Laderman: How, in spite of the culture?

Rainer: I do believe in retaining a certain marginal position, and shooting from the side. That isn't necessarily a matter of choice. My films have never been on PBS. They're too long and I really don't see that they could make it. In a way I'm proud of that, they're not assimilable in that way.

Laderman: So there are critical positions that people can take.

Rainer: It isn't only the strategy that makes things unpalatable. It's voices, who is using the strategies, who is talking. It's a matter of constant dialogue with what has been recuperated and the necessities of ongoing critique. This is never something fixed. I think the boundaries of political necessity are continually fluctuating. They're not rigid. Look at Godard's work and Kluge's recent work. There are very objectionable things within what are in other ways radical, critical films, mainly in the area of the way they deal with women. There are blind spots there. But we can still learn from them. They have had enormous impact in the way we think about society and our representation of it. And I'm sure in my films there are blind spots, lots of them. You could accuse some of the moments in *Film About a Woman Who...* of homophobia. But I've got to have faith that these films can be learned from, even if they don't follow traditional instructional formats.

Laderman: I have a sense that everything gets absorbed, everything is allowed for in our society right now.

Rainer: Not everything. There are always new areas of activism and real social pressures and crises that cause eruptions, like AIDS. Even though it's fashionable to take up AIDS as "social work," the demands of the young activists in ACT UP are emerging as an even broader critique of public health policies in this country.

Laderman: The video scene embodies the question of capitalist absorption. It's a medium that is in every middle-class household. On the other hand, it's used by a lot of avant-garde artists.

Rainer: And it's also used by activists.

Laderman: What about the impact of video on film? Film people see video as invading their art form.

Rainer: The ease with which optical effects can be achieved in video has produced a recapitulation or reenactment of early experimental or "underground" filmmaking. In that respect, video overly admires what technology can do, at the level of special effects. I have never been enamored of that way of looking or making for its own sake.

Laderman: Video seems to indicate the synthesis of pop culture and avant-garde strategies. Can you make a radical video and not have it dismissed as video?

Rainer: The word radical is key: what constitutes radical? Simply because you can produce an image upside down and inside out, what's the purpose of that kind of radicality?

Laderman: What strikes me so much about your films is their relation to the spectator, the form of address, how they interact with and try to provoke the spectator. What would you say you are trying to do to the spectator, what kind of interaction are you trying to produce, and do you see this as possibly relating to how people interact in society?

Rainer: I think I have much more modest aims than that question implies. I used to be more messianic than I am now, or the missionary zeal has shifted somewhat. I'm not sure what effect art has. It is obvious after the Rushdie debacle that art can have immense repercussions in society. But the kind of art I make I have no illusions about. I feel that artists can have an effect by organizing not only as artists but outside of being artists. I find that happening, other artists are doing that in ways I admire, like Martha Rosler, who is now curating a series of exhibits on housing and the homeless. An individual work of art, its only hope of having an effect is like a pebble in a pond, making contact with other pebbles, making ripples. At the moment of experience for the spectator, that can only be looked at as something not isolated but as part of an ongoing experience with certain kinds of work. That is the problem with distribution and exhibition. Usually it's a one-shot thing, it's looked on as an individual artistic expression, no matter how political the work is. It is a limitation of my films—one that I'm constantly dealing with and trying in very small ways to address, trying to get beyond the discussion of idiosyncratic formal techniques. Which in the early films is pretty much what people talk about. The social, ideological implications of that kind of discussion are very limited. I do have a great admiration for documentaries that do research in depth. I can never see myself doing a documentary on housing, but my last film deals with housing in a certain way. I continue to be a collagist and basically a fiction film maker. I don't know the effect. I do the kind of film I know how to do. All I can do is introduce more truth or more specificities in relation to real issues.

Laderman: We are so conditioned in the way we look at movies, with the Hollywood tradition being so dominant, when I watch a film like yours I feel like I'm being engaged in a totally different way.

Rainer: Yes, it's obvious that I want to engage you differently from the way Hollywood does it. But even that "evil empire" keeps changing. The seamless, illusionistic cinematic space is not the only one that the mass audience can handle. Which is not to say that there is not still a problem: how, in the fiction film, do you place individual lives in a social space, or in a space that invokes reality with as much vigor as fantasy?

Laderman: *El Norte* was the Hollywood version of the Guatemalan situation, and your version...

Rainer: I can't say I even made a version of that. *The Man Who Envied Women* presented the Guatemalan situation not only very fleetingly, but in relation to living in New York City in 1985. My films always return to a subjectivity in contention with itself as well as with social constraints. There are definite limitations to that. Maybe that's what my films are about, the struggle out of a paralyzing subjectivity. And, I would hope, a changing subjectivity.

David Laderman, while at San Francisco State University, wrote a Master's thesis on Yvonne Rainer's film, The Man Who Envied Women.

15

Barbara Hammer

Interviewed by Julia Hodges, Jamie Ramoneda,
and Kathy Sizeler

The non-linear, non-narrative progression of Barbara Hammer's work and her exploration of film and video technique require mental and physical participation from viewers. One of her main concerns is to transform the commonly passive position of the viewer into an active position that not only questions Hammer's intent as an artist but also questions the viewer's own ways of looking and responding. She is one of the leading forces in the gay and lesbian film movement and has been throughout her career involved in re-presenting lesbian and female experience. Hammer's visual language relies on a juxtaposition of images that refuses easy assimilation, drawing connections between sometimes difficult, sometimes mundane subjects and forcing the viewer to face his or her own prejudices, feelings, and fears. Her work uses inspirations from French psychoanalytic feminism, from gay pornography, and from the history of underground film, all in the service of a Brechtian intervention into the boundary-realm between society and art, creating there the estrangement from a repressive normality that is the condition for change. More than fifty of her short films and videos have been widely shown in festivals throughout the United States. Her first feature-length film, Nitrate Kisses, *premiered in 1992, shortly after this 1991 interview.* Nitrate Kisses *uses both new and found footage, and draws upon the tradition of gay pornography.*

Julia Hodges/Jamie Ramoneda/Kathy Sizeler: In your development as a feminist, experimental filmmaker, and throughout your career, who has influenced you and in what ways?

Barbara Hammer: I have been influenced throughout my "career," if one can call the neglected backwaters of experimental filmmaking a career, by various filmmakers, philosophies, and people. I believe I am and have been told that I am a very impressionable person, so I expect those films and filmmakers who have inspired or challenged me to have a great influence on my work and its development. The first film I saw somewhere between three and five years of age was Walt Disney's *Bambi*. I asked my mother, "Who's turning the pages?" and I was terrified during the fire scene. Very early I learned the literary bias and the violent nature of Hollywood cinema. Perhaps I was "saved" from Hollywood, the city I was born in, by the depression and my parents' small income.

When I was twenty-one, while I was in the first years of an aborted marriage, I saw *Pather Panchali* by Satyajit Ray and was introduced into a world of filmmaking beyond Hollywood. After that marvelous black and white film that transported me to another culture and other ways of seeing and thinking, I preferred the small art houses that ran the subtitled films because there were more ideas and challenging world views. I was already tired of the plot-point trap that Hollywood screenwriting dictates.

Six years later, I was an English teacher for "emotionally disturbed" adolescents in a juvenile hall, in the process of burning out on a three-year floor-to-ceiling house building experience in the Sonoma County woods, a nine-year marriage, and teaching. I wanted to create. I studied painting with William Morehouse. He brought a leather-clad woman model with her motorcycle into the class, and I was so inspired I stretched the largest canvas yet, and in an attempt to show the movement I felt her figure implied, gave her extra arms, hands, legs, and feet. Later I painted with materials that would change under varying lights and constructed color wheels or black light paintings that moved while viewed.

A major change occurred when Bill brought in an old Kodak 16mm projector able to work at varying speeds and some clear

16mm film leader for me to paint on. That was the day I became a filmmaker. I painted on the film using a glaze paint made for aquariums that crystallized when it dried, and constructed a mirror box of four sides in which to project. My first developed film was re-photography, as I set up a camera to film the projected kaleidoscope in the mirrors. (Little could I imagine that twenty-five years later I would be making a four-screen film with an optical printer.) Someone gave me a Super 8mm Bolex, and I was off and running, literally, through the closest town, Bodega, filming my shadow, cobwebs through bifocal lenses the optometrist gave me, and attaching the psychedelic footage of the handpainted crystals. *Schizy* (1968) was my first film. Two things happened with that film that helped me to continue in filmmaking: it won an Honorable Mention at the Sonoma County 8mm Film Festival, and the experience of watching it projected with an audience was incredible. The film was larger than any canvas I'd painted and the audience was captured by the darkness and direction of light to watch my work in a way no one had looked at my paintings. That was it. I was a filmmaker.

I continued to make 8 and Super 8mm films but it wasn't until 1972 when I was enrolled in film history class and saw *Meshes of the Afternoon* by Maya Deren that I knew there was room for a woman's vision on the screen. I believe I recognized gender construction and projection in that film, although I didn't have the language more than "woman's imagery" at that time. My first 16mm film, *I Was I Am,* pays direct homage to Deren. Not only am I the protagonist, I go through a transformation from a princess to a dyke, and after discarding my tiara take a key from my mouth to start the engine on my motorcycle; but also, many of the films of the '70s, especially *The Psychosynthesis Trilogy (I Was I Am,* 1973; *X,* 1974; and *Psychosynthesis,* 1975), are replete with charged imagery that represents for me emotional meanings.

Deren as a theorist was also important. *Film Culture,* No. 39, Winter 1965 included many of her writings. Especially important to me was her description of "vertical cinema" as opposed to a horizontal, linear, often narrative cinema. The sense of image relation building on image relation in a deep, impacted manner of possibilities and ambiguities made cinema a wealthy field for me. The "brick-building" theory of cinema of accumulation in a narrow and straight line never appealed to me, as life seemed so much more complex, my emotions so multiple, and mystery more important than "scientific understanding."

So it was no wonder that when *New French Feminisms,* edited by Elaine Marks and Isabelle de Courtivron, published "This Sex Which Is Not One" by Luce Irigaray in 1981 I was captivated by her creative and wondrous writing of the multiplicity of woman's sexuality. Woman with her two genital lips is already two according to Irigaray, two who stimulate and embrace continually and who are not divisible into ones. This idea, so poetically expressed, reinforced my desire to express myself in multiple images either through superimpositions, bi-packing of two or more images in the optical printer, or passing the film through the printer various times. Never was I trying to "veil" a meaning, but rather to enlarge upon a feeling/tone I was creating.

Teresa de Lauretis in *Alice Doesn't* (1982) and *Technologies of Gender* (1987) opens the doors of semiotic and structural criticism to feminist theory based on experience. For the first time the referent, i.e., the subject, can return to a post-post-modern discourse as de Lauretis makes a wedge for the self-representation of difference outside, I believe, the bipolarity of gender dictated by a heterosexist ideology. In other words, the lesbian stands both within and outside of gender representation, and we can turn to her works of self-representation for the "third gender." Feminists have recognized the difference in a black woman's experience from a white woman's and that most discourse until recently has been written from a white woman's perspective. Similarly, the lesbian experience has been wrongly subsumed in a heterosexist discourse. De Lauretis suggests the off-screen space as cracks in a heterosexist hegemony from which the voice(s) of difference can begin to speak.

Although I didn't have the theory or the words to form it, I worked throughout the '70s to make films of my lesbian experience. These stand outside the heterosexual discourse on gender and its representation. I was propelled in numerous films to "represent one lesbian identity/experience" by making images that were unique to my re-naming myself as lesbian. I believed that in making films that re-presented at least one lesbian's experience (my own as I knew no other), I could contribute to abolishing lesbian invisibility.

Maya Deren, Luce Irigaray, and Teresa de Lauretis have in their writings and in Deren's case filmmaking as well, confirmed my intuitive creative processes and have helped give me words to name my endeavors. I find that reading and re-reading them sustains and propels me in a community of discourse.

Hodges/Ramoneda/Sizeler: How have you affected other women filmmakers? How have you helped to pave the way for women and feminists in experimental film?

Hammer: I don't know exactly how I have affected other women filmmakers, although I have seen bright, excited, and inspired faces in an audience after a presentation. I have thanks and gratitude for the images and the discussion that followed them. Sometimes I get letters from women who tell me how important my work has been for them. Sometimes I get silence.

It is difficult for me to say how I have helped to pave the way for women and feminists in experimental film. History provided the conjunction of theory with my artistic production. I did find an experimental film-going audience devoid of feminist theory and practice and, similarly, a feminist audience that knew little about the inquiry of experimental cinema. I have tried in personal presentations to address these issues by talking about the importance and contributions of feminism to an audience of avant-garde film lovers and about the viability and expansion of possibilities that experimental cinema provides a feminist audience.

Today the discourse is more defined. After a recent Lesbian and Gay Experimental Film Festival a young gay filmmaker said he didn't understand why my early '70s films were critiqued for not including much representation of women of different ethnic backgrounds. We would be forcing ourselves to fulfill a formula of political correctness, he thought, to be all-inclusive. Wrong, I said, it is up to us to expand our personal experience beyond a limited one-dimensional whiteness.

Hodges/Ramoneda/Sizeler: Your recent films are characterized by non-linear, non-narrative multiple images which you manipulate in various ways. How would you respond to someone who says, "All I see is pretty pictures"?

Hammer: If someone responded to me after seeing my films that all they saw were "pretty pictures," I'd have to respond that they didn't see my films. Of course, every film has a different intention and result, but primarily I am concerned with stimulating multiple perceptual inputs simultaneously to engage the viewer in active participation to determine meaning. Meaning may be emotional, intellectual, or a perceptual knowledge based on visuals, rhythm, frame, or shot duration and composition, sound/image relationship. I am asking a lot of the viewer: to be awake to simultaneous input in many sensory and intellectual areas. And, to put them altogether in a synthesis of understanding. The guidelines are within the interception of the text, i.e., the film, and the viewer's reading.

Hodges/Ramoneda/Sizeler: Who is your audience, and has it changed in response to your work? Do you feel responsible for providing your audience with the tools necessary to understand your (visual) language?

Hammer: My audience has changed somewhat with the change of direction I've taken in my films. Although this isn't always the case, generally my audience has become more aficionados of the avant-garde filmic genre than the lesbians and/or feminists that populated the theaters in the '70s. An amazing and growing exception to this is the mixed audience in New York City attending the Experimental Lesbian and Gay Film Festival that is in its fifth remarkable year of a week-long series of mostly sold-out programs of gay and lesbian experimental cinema. The audience there is demanding, appreciative, and knows quality of intention and finish in first films by emerging filmmakers, as well as those of us who have been engaged in production for many years. This festival has given an impetus to lesbian and gay experimental filmmakers to keep working (some filmmakers make films each year expressly for the festival) because they know they have an opportunity for exhibition.

I'm sorry to say this hasn't always been the case. My lesbian films were often rejected by avant-garde showcases across the county and in museums everywhere during the period I was actively and expressly engaged in making lesbian representation. It wasn't until I "depopulated" my cinema, i.e., took the women out, that I began to get the invitations I had so long sought after. Believe me there were calluses on my knuckles from knocking at locked doors, for I am not one to accept a "no" and go away quietly.

There has been a social control or censorship as well that has worked against the exhibition of my lesbian films. Once in the Tri Cities area of the South, the church fathers closed their doors and withdrew their permission for the screening of *Dyketactics* and *Multiple Orgasm*. A few years ago I was met at the Buffalo, New York, airport by a worried curator who informed me that the "vice squad" was waiting at the local gallery to pre-screen the films to make sure they weren't pornographic. I had the choice to refuse to screen them and disappoint a community audience of 200 or sit there chagrined and mortified while these two men looked for any "child nudity" or "abuse of men" as they defined pornography. I chose the latter, and it was very difficult. I showed them the most graphic of the films, although I was mortified through every minute of the projection. That evening they came to the screening at the club and commented that *Superdyke* contained child pornography, as there were two nude prepubescent girls in the film. I pointed out that those girls were holding the hand of their also nude mother and that was consent. Furthermore, they were all walking through a field of grass. The film was celebratory of a new found independence and freedom from social restriction, yet here I was caught in the clutches of a police mentality upholding a foreign and secretly coded morality. No person should have to undergo the humiliation of censorship. I would never do it again.

I do feel responsible for providing my audience with the tools necessary to understand my visual language, but not by taking them by the hand and leading them one by one through the images or formal construction of the film. Rather, I like to present what some of my concerns were in making the film that suggest a language. That allows the audience to work however they want to participate in the code or references I use without limiting their experience to mine.

As there are feminisms not feminism, so there are multiple ways of knowing just about everything. I think the future of the planet and all that entails means an increased ability to function and comprehend on multiple layers and ways of knowing at the same time. This challenges the old mode of "do one thing at a time." Just as light can be understood by both a wave and a particle theory, so too can the juxtaposition of imagery, rhythms, color and black/white have multiple meanings. Openness of readings is what I'm looking for in my audience, not closures.

Hodges/Ramoneda/Sizeler: In creating a language or sign-system for women and/or lesbians, are you avoiding naming and defining, or are you renaming?

Hammer: Until recently lesbians were unnamed in film, on radio, in the popular press. At most, we were named historically by patriarchal medicalizations. I was thirty years old when I first heard the word "lesbian." That word wasn't heard or written until the second wave of feminism in the 1970s. With the word came a change of lifestyles for many of us who immediately or slowly recognized emotional, sexual, and physical attractions to women. Some women I'm sure are more precocious than me, but it took the name, the "L" word, for me to rename myself and act on hitherto unnamed desire. Amazing. Until there is a naming and a construction there can't be a deconstruction. So I think that during the '70s we were naming ourselves; it was a community affair. Now in the '90s we can deconstruct the social identity we gave ourselves. With that ability to reexamine we can then re-construct with greater consciousness and permission what self-representation we desire.

Hodges/Ramoneda/Sizeler: What role does sexuality and desire play in creating this discourse?

Hammer: Our experience of sexuality and desire changes, and with those changes comes a change in discourse. For example, with the newly found expression of our charged sexuality unleashed, so to speak, from the unconscious past, many of us ran headlong and passionately from one woman to the next. What we named "uninhibited activity" and "sexual freedom" could later be renamed as "love addiction" or "dyke drama." We are a new and changing community, and the discourse matures as we mature. The depth of love expressed through longevity and commitment of lesbians in daily relations that continually self-define without guarantees is the challenging position where I find myself at fifty-one, or put another way, a twenty-one-year-old lesbian practitioner.

Hodges/Ramoneda/Sizeler: How can you say that your discourse in film is a women's language?

Hammer: I can say that my discourse in film is a woman's language because of my experience of being a woman. The trick is that the constructed language is often a man's language, but the way in which it is used can be very womanly. Similarly, as a lesbian woman and as a lesbian woman experimental filmmaker, my experiences are different and the images, juxtapositions, abstractions, rhythms, and textures will state that difference.

Hodges/Ramoneda/Sizeler: Do you feel that labelling yourself as 1)experimental 2) lesbian film artist limits your work or audience in any way?

Hammer: Yes, probably my label of myself as experimental and as lesbian film artist limits my audience more than my work, as I seem to go ahead and make what I want to make without any other than my own personal limitations. Both experimental film and lesbian film are endangered categories, and as long as that is the case it is necessary to name them. Without a name and without activity of self-definition they will go away, dissolve into the mainstream, exist in hiding. It is a political act to name and be named and to name again and that will be so until we truly exist in an egalitarian world with an inquiring population.

Hodges/Ramoneda/Sizeler: Can this marginal discourse reach the mainstream and have any effect on the dominant patriarchal discourse? Should it? What effect, if any, are you trying to have on the mainstream discourse? If your films became part of the mainstream, would they lose their impact?

Hammer: Most marginal discourses reach the mainstream in this novelty-hungry capitalist society, and parts and pieces reappear in the popular press or commercial movies in a newly renovated and camouflaged avant-garde image. Agents and imagemongers, garbage collectors rummaging the downtown scene, the newly acquired films at the archive, the new hybrid genres that appear are grabbed in a flash only to re-emerge in a Calvin Klein bus stop ad or a 2 billion dollar budgeted film script. I am not trying to have an effect on the mainstream discourse, but by reason of my making work and putting it out I and other film and video artists will possibly in some manner have our work appropriated. At that time we will inscribe new margins for our free expression until we are reincorporated and on and on and so the process goes. The avant-garde can never really be appropriated, for the style and gestures do not the person make. The grit, the anguish, the *jouissance* or bliss, the human passions, and intellectual struggles behind the imagery remain a secret to the surface collector who spatters paint after Jackson Pollock on a T-shirt.

Hodges/Ramoneda/Sizeler: In a previous interview, you expressed a desire to increase the audience's awareness of their own bodies by creating a tactile sensation from visual stimuli. Could you talk about how this makes an audience more active? Is this attempt to encourage perception beyond the visual, in a mostly visual art, an effort to subvert the mainstream?

Hammer: The effort to kinaesthetically "touch" my audience through visual stimuli so that they "feel" the images in their bodies grew from a personal recognition to a political strategy. I noticed a developed sensate link between some things I looked at in the natural world. For example, driving along a plowed field I, while looking, would also feel the texture of the earth in rows within my body as a generalized feeling sensation. I look at a polished hardwood floor and literally "feel" the hardness and smoothness interiorly. I began to poll my audiences to see if other people had a similar response. Only a few would raise their hands or nod in agreement. I thought most didn't know what I was talking about so I began decidedly to construct and to create these "feeling" images. I think that if people are more aware of physical sensations in general they are more active in the physical world of politics, for example. On the smallest scale to vote is a physical activity, on a larger scale to organize and demonstrate is a huge bodily effort, and to commit to change can be a totally consuming physical experience. I must directly confront stasis if I am to challenge the passivity of the entertained audience in a mainstream linear film where plot-points appear and change the script as regularly as a clock.

The audience swims in *Pond and Waterfall.* The still body of the audience was to be enveloped in a pond of water moving slowly about, then faster down a stream and eventually over a waterfall and out into the ocean. Swimming the camera I would swim the audience so they would not only appreciate the pristine and unique nature of an eco-system but also recognize their personal and physiological containment as a blood-coursing, oxygen-using self-sufficient and codependent system. The film is silent so they can hear their own heartbeat and fluids coursing much as one hears the pressure system of the pond's weight underwater. My idea is that an activated and physically stimulated audience is more likely to engage in the world outside the theater in an active manner than a passive observer who moves from theater to world as in a dream. I want us to change the way the systems are, politics operates, people oppress. I do not want to replicate a model of conformity and passivity.

Hodges/Ramoneda/Sizeler: You once said that men and women probably have a genetic difference in perception due to the xx and xy chromosomes. Do you still think this is true?

Hammer: I really don't know if chromosomal difference could lead to perceptual differences. It might. It might not. In an attempt to know, it would be impossible, I think, to separate learned and constructed gender perceptions from biological tendencies. Probably a multiple reading of differences from all levels of understanding would be the model I'd subscribe to now. Class, race, sexual preference, age, physicalism, as well as chromosomes could all inscribe difference.

Hodges/Ramoneda/Sizeler: How would you characterize your work's transformation from bodies of humans (women) to bodies of land (geography)? What prompted this change from interior to exterior?

Hammer: One of the reasons that I began to make exterior films of the landscape in the '80s was to expand the language from the interior, body-focused imagery to the world. I did not want to work on language that could only speak from the enclosed space of my body. Women have been defined by their bodies and their domestic spaces for too long. I want to expand that projection. I wanted to walk the world with my camera, expressing physical concepts of "bent time," the curving of time at the edge of the universe as noted by physicists (*Bent Time,* 1984); architectural space as both two and three dimensional as well as experimental (*Pools,* 1981); and the fragile material nature of film (*Endangered,* 1988).

In *Still Point* (1989) I return to the body but this time in conjunction with the exterior world. The screen is divided into four spaces: two domestic scenes and two scenes of homeless street people. My lover and I are seen meeting at the airport, hiking across an empty volcano in Hawaii, playing with our food while homeless people beg for money, pick out aluminum cans from garbage pails, and sleep in the park. It is important that our discourse move to include others while not neglecting the significance of personal relationships. At the same time two lesbian women are courting and developing a life together, two or more other people are without necessary amenities for minimum life requirements. We are important; all of us are important.

Hodges/Ramoneda/Sizeler: Discuss your move to create an alternative discourse that is not tied to the body. Why is this important?

Hammer: It is important to the survival of all of us that we keep and respect our differences, protect ourselves and others from the many threats to all forms of life, and collectively clean up our act on this planet. As experimental filmmakers, as lesbians and gay men, as feminists and socialists, as people of color and people without color, we must reach beyond our borders and address the issues of survival that face us in the late twentieth century.

Hodges/Ramoneda/Sizeler: Where do you see your work going in the future?

Hammer: Where is my work going in the future? Presently I am interested in remembering forgotten footage, women and men from film history, and particular cinematic concerns that have lain dormant. While touring the archive at the George Eastman House in Rochester, New York, I saw a number of silver cans marked "Watson's X-Rays." That site of discovering has led to *Sanctus,* a film using x-ray footage of the moving human body skeleton and interiors shot by Dr. James Sibly Watson and collaborators in the 1950s. With the soundtrack by Niel B. Rolnick who digitized the "Sanctus" section of the mass from recordings by Beethoven, Bach, Mozart, Byrd, the viewer enters the invisible, the place unseen yet familiar, his/her body. The "holy" body. The fragile body. The experimental body. I have returned to the interior body but through the exterior remains of the first cinefluorographic motion pictures of the human skeleton and organs. As we rush into the future it behooves us to look at our history. To stop, digest, inhale, read, and reflect. To appreciate and respect; to despair and vow never to repeat. It is a time for contemplation, pause, and evaluation. I hope this for my work, that it becomes more reflective, considered, and thoughtful.

Julia Hodges works for Red Bass *magazine; Jamie Ramoneda is a poet; and Kathy Sizeler is a visual artist. All reside in New Orleans, Louisiana.*

16

Ida Applebroog

Interviewed by Xenia Zed

Since her editions of small, powerful bookworks in the '70s, Ida Applebroog's voice has been a constant aesthetic and moral presence in the world of contemporary art. Her newer paintings, multiple panel works, and installations continue to explore themes of violence, injustice, domestic politics, and social forces with insight, wit, and intellectual depth. The dramatic visual presence of her works was amply demonstrated in 1990, the year in which this conversation took place, with an exhibition that surveyed fifteen years of her work, "Ida Applebroog: Happy Families," organized by the Contemporary Arts Museum in Houston. She was also one of the most talked about artists in the controversial 1993 Whitney Biennial. Her paintings do not adopt the straightforward political outrage that characterizes the work of, for example, Leon Golub. She captures perfectly the horrors and the ambiguities, the passion for justice and the pressure of despair in the contemporary human situation. She is a voice in the wilderness, and her honesty about the realities and the sources of the miseries we visit upon each other raises her work to a high ethical and artistic plane. It is her clear, pessimistic vision, accompanied by an undeniable hope for a human future, that aligns her work with the interventionists and provocateurs in this volume.

Xenia Zed: What question do you get tired of answering and what question do you wish someone would ask ?

Ida Applebroog: I don't really expose myself in that way to the public, so questions I'm asked a lot are usually students' questions: "Do you think that your work is political or it's going to change the world?" Of course I'm not that naive; I know that there's no way that my art or anything I do or say is going to change the world. Much of my own political activism is outside of my artwork. I do hope that whatever I have to say in my art is said for a reason, and at least may serve to make some people think more. That's the question I get asked at every gig I do, the first question that comes up. I also get an awful lot of questions about the art market today, but I wish I would be asked about why I am an artist, why am I doing it, what makes me be an artist. For some reason that sort of slips out of the questioning process.

Zed: You once said that in the '70s, people didn't talk about art and money, they talked about art, and it seems in the '80s now we're back to talking about art and money.

Applebroog: The '70s was a very different time; we were coming out of Vietnam, the flower children, and feminism, and that was the real world out there. The art world itself, it was all isms—minimalism, conceptualism, site works, earth works, performances. I came to New York in the mid-'70s, and the dealers actually moved into SoHo to accommodate all the large works. It changed in the '80s, the age of Reaganism, and now we're back to tradition and back to the basics. And the '80s were really about money, about yuppies and the artworld as a marketplace. We're talking about price tags, we're not talking about art.

Zed: How do you feel about inevitably being a part of that system, dealing in part with ideas that deconstruct kind of a politics of power in your work and then having that stuck back into a system that's all about power and about art as a better investment than real estate?

Applebroog: Look, that's reality, and I'm not going to knock the idea of that. You remember going all the way back to the '40s and '50s, no artist thought about money, the '60s and '70s, no art student thought about money. Everyone who went out to be an artist knew that they had to figure out a way to make a living outside their art. Teaching was one way, or you worked at a museum, or as a waitress, or you did any number of other things, but you did not expect to make money out of your art. Now I think I would be rather stupid to feel that it's so terrible to make money through my art. Now, after editing, after teaching, after all those things that took me away from my art, I'm now being paid for my work. So if I said anything other than that I'd be a liar. It's a problem, it's a real problem. I can talk against the system, but I'm just telling you how I feel personally. The system is a very flawed system; when you talk about Van Gogh's *Irises* going for fifty-four million dollars at auction you get to the point where you wonder whether the work is really so priceless. People can't really look at the work anymore without thnking about the price.

Zed: Well, perhaps in the '90s there will be a sort of solution to that dilemma of the object that represents so many ideas and conveys so many messages being locked away in a vault, ceasing to serve the purpose dealt to it.

Applebroog: Do you really think it is going to get better in the '90s? My prediction for the '90s is that museums will have all these precious objects worth so much money in vaults, and what you're going to be looking at on the walls is copies of those paintings. I mean, that's a funny idea, but it's not that unreal of an idea.

Zed: Well, it's happening with the caves of Lascaux.

Applebroog: And also if you go to Monet Gardens, you can buy copies of any Monet painting you like. It's even one step further.

Zed: Anonymity seems to be very important to you—being apart from or aside from circumstances, not going out into the world but choosing to be with artists in the world, not wanting to talk about meaning explicitly in your paintings because that may affect the interpretation that the individual will have of your work. Could you talk about that?

Applebroog: Well, you actually just talked about it. I don't think my ideas are of major importance. Art should be able to stand on its own. Biographical information should not inform us as to what the piece is about. If it doesn't stand on its own it's just not worth dealing with.

Zed: Do you feel that any biographical information detracts from the work?

Applebroog: Yes, I do. I really do. I find that if I leave the work ambiguous enough people come in and interpret it their own way. You may have six different reviews coming out over the same period of time, and each one will interpret the work totally differently.

Zed: You have talked about your work, that you would like for your work to be kind of a projective series of tests, like Rorschach tests. Are you interested in the Rorschach readings? Have you collected any of those readings or has that fed into your work in any way? How do you feel about the various interpretations and responses that your work receives?

Applebroog: Once your work goes out there, you have no choice. The interpretation has begun to be made, whether it's by someone who feels the same way you do or by someone who is a total conservative. You might have this reactionary person loving that piece of work and taking it very seriously because he is interpreting it on a different level. What are you supposed to do with that work? Take the work back and say, no you can't look at it, I only want people to look at it who will agree with the way I think about it? I don't want to change anyone's interpretation of it. People learn to react from where they come from and it has nothing to do with what I say or my interpretation. I use everyday objects and everyday people, normal people, common people, generic people...

Zed: But is there such a thing as a generic person? It seems that trying so hard to depict the generic person blasts us with the fact that there is no such thing.

Applebroog: But that's the idea. When you see a generic product in the store that has no ad that goes with it, you can read into it anything you want. In a way, people take their identity with them in their little bag. That's why I talk about generic people. It's a way of saying, O.K., this can be anybody.

Zed: But, it's almost impossible for it not to be yourself.

Applebroog: Well, it has to be, and the funny part of it is of course, as a female, I come to the work with a whole set of experiences, so that the way I present these people is entirely different from this other person who just happens to be male.

Zed: In hearing different interpretations of your work, have you noticed any distinction between the male point of view and the female point of view?

Applebroog: It's hard to tell. I think that you can't help that. It's built into almost any work whether you're male or female. It's a lot different when you're writing; you have female writers and male writers. Supposedly, the males always write about the universal condition. Women will be actually writing the same thing, writing about the universal condition—but for them, it will be labelled as writing women's problems. When reading a piece of writing you think, is this a woman talking or is this a man talking? It's a very different interpretation. Male artists are never made to worry about their gender as a creative negative.

Zed: What are your observations about women who assume kind of the persona of the male in public in order to make their statements and women who realize this and refuse to do it, by working small, dealing with the intimacies of daily life versus the universal view? Do you have any comments on that? Has it changed any from the '60s and the '70s to the '80s?

Applebroog: It has changed in the '80s. When pattern and decoration was so big in the '70s, you didn't think of the big names associated with it. Pattern and decoration comes out of the feminist movement, yet you hardly ever hear the names of the women that were associated with it.

Zed: It seems to me that pattern and decoration just died, it was dropped. It was never carried out to the end or pressed beyond its original boundary.

Applebroog: We're talking about money and politics again. In the '80s, Schnabel and the young heroic male painters came along.

Zed: Do you think there's any way to get around that?

Applebroog: There never has been before, I mean these things just go around and around, and if you wait long enough, you'll be in there for the next round. It's a matter of patience and pre-vailing—not just surviving.

Zed: It seems to me when looking at your work, that you don't depict emotion as much as you utilize emotion as a tool—that underneath the surface there's always this emotional charge that's used as an element of construction. That emotion, in a sense, becomes your paintbrush.

Applebroog: I'm not quite sure it's unconscious like that.

Zed: Susan Krane, in her catalogue essay, says, "Applebroog, in many ways, is a social realist who looks at humanity from the inside out rather than the outside in." How do you feel about that?

Applebroog: It's pretty accurate. I come to these works with a certain amount of information and who I am, and that's all. The information is from the outside—I take the information inside and then have it come outside again. I think we all work inside/outside all the time at all levels.

Zed: You talked about your hope that in these paintings there would be a chaos of possibilities. What would some of those possibilities be?

Applebroog: I think that's for the viewer to figure out. All I do is take all the ideas and put them all together—it's like they're impacted images for the viewer to pull apart and hopefully someone out there will get something out of it. Sometimes you don't get anything out of it. There are times when people walk away from a certain piece and scratch their heads, and that's okay, too.

Zed: Your work has been described as dealing with the psychopathology of everyday life.

Applebroog: Yes, but those are not my words, those are Freud's words.

Zed: It is hard for me to objectify the emotions that I find in your work and the issues that you deal with. That seems tremendously ironic because the work is so incredibly loaded and so difficult to talk about without refering to the personal, even though there's a universality to it.

Applebroog: Well I wish that I could give you a formula or a recipe but I can't.

Zed: I'm not looking for a formula or a recipe—but, Linda McGreevy, who talked about the dilemma of the critic in discussing these works, described a sense of not showing your emotions, not being emotional. I think that's kind of shown up everywhere in society.

Applebroog: Oh yes, and unemotional art is very distant, it's very cool, it's about media technology and it's very male. There are a couple of women who have been allowed into this nice circle. But many women are doing very interesting work, but you just don't hear about them. The wonderful thing about technology is that technology takes over. We're living in the media age.

Zed: Why is that wonderful?

Applebroog: Well, I think it's wonderful for the whole population out there. I mean we're talking about things like televangelism. We just finished with an actor president, Star Wars technology, Calvin Klein. We seem to want that. This is the age we live in. This is what we're used to. This is what the kids are being brought up on and so when art does the same thing it's wonderful. It fits right in.

Zed: Well, we have the perfect little module that is kind of self-encapsulated, like a pill for everyone to swallow. What's your prediction on that?

Applebroog: I'm afraid I'm not into predictions. My way is that I hope for the best. Life goes on eventually and I work for the next cycle to start.

Zed: When you make a reference in your work, how does that work? I'm not even sure how to ask the question. I don't think that the Holocaust can become a metaphor in the sense that the Holocaust is the Holocaust and always will be. But, I'm interested in the connection there. Could you talk about that?

Applebroog: It's a personal connection and it's something that is with me all of my life and I will never be able to separate it out. We're talking about the representation of mass psychosis; we're also talking about individual psychosis.

Zed: So this, in a sense, is a collective memory that will never go away, and it is the harbinger of that possibly occuring again. How did the image of the Holocaust come about in *The Crimson Garden*, which was originally titled *The Auschwitz Gardens*?

Applebroog: I come to the work with a kind of an idea and here it was the idea of Auschwitz and all its horrors. I hope that if the idea works, it ends up being read into the entire piece.

Zed: What about the relationship of landscape, landscape as a backdrop?

Applebroog: That actually started in 1986. That was the first time I introduced landscape. I have a place upstate in the country.

I go there every year in the summer, and somehow it must have come through. Until then I always worked in the city. I guess it sort of seeped in very slowly and suddenly I realized I was doing landscape, and they are surreal. They are not based on trying to do some place I saw.

Zed: What about the statement, "It's what isn't being said that can't be represented"?

Applebroog: You know this work is always about silence. I use text a lot and the images of silence are about what isn't being said.

Zed: It seems that in the video *Belladonna* you were far more specific about issues and references than you are in your paintings.

Applebroog: Yes, it's because it's a different medium. You are taking these talking heads and blowing them up to monumental proportions. You should be surrounded by the low tone. You should be surrounded by the voices. They should not be coming in the way you would experience television. They should be all around you.

Zed: In *Art News*, Ruth Bass said that oftentimes you do not realize the implications of your paintings until long after you have created them. You've had two or four years to think about these paintings. Have the implications changed for you since the time you first created them?

Applebroog: I tend to do the works and then I have to sort of resurrect them for each show. I have to look at them again. It's very hard. I do them. They are finished. They are gone. Sometimes they'll sit in the studio for a year and somewhere in there in that year I live with the work, something will occur to me and I figure out why I did that and feel exposed. But that only happens in a very short period of about a year, and then after that if they are showing at my gallery or if they are showing elsewhere I'll go to the opening. I'll look at the work but I don't see it anymore.

Zed: What are you working on now?

Applebroog: In the new work there is a great deal of medical content and medical terminology.

Zed: The paintings here that have specific medical references, *K-Mart Village I* and *K-Mart Village II*, seem to deal with ageism and the frustrations of a person in midlife having to deal with an aging parent. Why K-Mart?

Applebroog: It's part of the American ethos. How could I not use K-Mart?

Zed: But K-Mart in connection with a surgeon. Well, I guess it's really getting to be more and more and that way. All these questions I've asked you, you've sort of answered indirectly, but that's fine. The chaos of the unnameable possibilities...how do you feel when someone says, looking at your work, that it is impossible not to flinch?

Applebroog: I never quite understand that.

Zed: Well it's because the paintings are so confrontational. Because there's so much mastery in drawing the viewer into the situation of the paintings, it's almost like a venus flytrap. In a sense, the images are almost innocuous at first glance. The faces are blank, the images are familiar. But then, of course, after you spend a few moments longer you realize that you, yourself, are implicated in making those assumptions and you flinch. It is also true with the books, the flip books, the pet performances...

Applebroog: Yes well, the books I understand. I mailed them out and got some very negative responses—"Please do not send me any more of those books, how dare you intrude."—it's the idea of infringing on their right to privacy. I don't want to do that. At that point it occurred to me—or the occurrence was thrown into my face—that I'd made some people very uncomfortable.

Zed: Did you anticipate that? You didn't anticipate it.

Applebroog: No, I mean it's the art world, where you just do your thing. It never occured to me that they would respond like that.

Zed: Isn't it wonderful how they've become so collectible now?

Applebroog: In a way I guess. It was a funny joke at first. I had a batch of books and I numbered all of them. I had these disposable objects and I wanted to get away from preciousness. At the very end after I had numbered the last book, they all had the same number, which made them totally useless as a collector's item. The number didn't mean anything.

Zed: What do you think has happened to women artists in the '80s and what do you think is going to happen to women artists in the '90s?

Applebroog: Well I think we came a very long way in the '70s and lost quite a bit in the early '80s. I mean take the museum shows, for example. I'm not that familiar with the statistics but the numbers didn't look good. In the feminist movement, after the '70s, we thought there was this whole new generation coming up and they would take over, but indeed it wasn't that way. The new generation came up and felt there was no problem, because they were getting into shows and they were being represented. But at the end of the '70s and into the '80s many of the women were being dropped. I remember the Museum of Modern Art had a survey on recent painting and sculpture with ninety-five men and fourteen women. It was a turning point. I happened to know all the women in the show but that didn't change our real anger and the rage that we had lost so much ground. I felt we were almost back to square one. It happened in the corporate world also. All these young women coming into corporate jobs thinking, "Well, of course I can get a job, I can get as much pay as a man; I can move right up the corporate ladder." They kept going and they just couldn't get those positions and they were not making as much money as the men and they also became somewhat radicalized. It's interesting in relation to the abortion issue. I went to the big Pro-Choice demonstration in Washington, D.C., and I was shocked. Here in Washington, D.C., there were all these different women on the plane, taking the shuttle with me. Corporate women with their attache cases. A lot of religious people for choice, nuns for choice, and it felt very nice because I realized we weren't just the radical fringe anymore. There are women out there who are very interested because it has to do with them as women. I think it's going to change. I think it has changed. I am tremendously hopeful about what's happening to women.

Zed: Do you foresee any specific pitfalls for women artists and the women's movement?

Applebroog: I don't know. I really hope that we can stay on a very hopeful note and just keep fighting and not think about the bad parts. Keep punching. Try hard not to think about the worst scenario, but the best.

Zed: What is your hope for your work from this point on in terms of what you want to do with it?

Applebroog: Keep on living and working. I can't do any more than that.

Zed: I want to ask you one more question that you may not want to answer but I'll ask it anyway. And that is, I read an account of your name, sort of the birthing of your name, and I wondered what Applebroog signifies for you now, or what it signified at the time of its birth.

Applebroog: You're right; I don't want to answer that.

Xenia Zed *is an artist and former editor of* Art Papers.

17

Nina Menkes

Interviewed by Linda M. Brooks

The work of experimental filmmaker Nina Menkes has been described as "powerful and extraordinary" as well as "controversial, intense, and visually stunning." Her first feature, The Great Sadness of Zohara, *on a young woman's anguished journey through the deserts of Israel and Africa, was shown in Paris, Munich, and Beijing in 1986. Her second film,* Magdalena Viraga, *on a prostitute's self-hatred, her false arrest for murder, and her final apotheosis as a gentle, black-winged witch, won the L.A. Film Critic's Association Award and toured throughout Europe, Asia, and the U.S.* Queen of Diamonds, *released in 1991, the year before this interview took place, is about a woman blackjack dealer in Las Vegas. The film won an American Film Institute award in addition to support from the National Endowment for the Arts. It played to enthusiastic audiences at the Sundance Festival in Utah and the AFI Festival in Washington, D.C., and was chosen to open the 1991 Munich International Film Festival. Described by the L.A. Times critic Kevin Thomas as "taxing, shimmering, and hypnotic,"* Queen of Diamonds *is difficult and rewarding. Her most recent film,* The Bloody Child, *released in 1996, hypnotically depicts a spreading desolation in the wake of domestic violence. Her work is less explicitly political than most of the artists collected in this volume, yet her uncompromising representation of the lives of women in postindustrial capitalism achieves a true vision of modern life that is inherently provocational. It is in her ability to bring difficult truths and ideas to the foreground of her highly suggestive films that we can see the tactical and postutopian character of her work.*

Linda Brooks: How did you become interested in film?

Nina Menkes: Well, I guess it started when I was a teenager. I was a dancer and a choreographer until I had a bad knee injury. Every time I would get to a point of competence I would have problems with it. But I did love choreography. I was living in London with a few other dancers. And I had an idea for a dance film. I don't really know where I got the idea for film. I think it was actually because my great aunt gave me this Super 8 camera and I thought we would make a little dance film. For fun. And then one of my roommates, whose friend was involved in a film school in London and who had no idea what to do for his film, suggested that he do my idea, basically, and I would just do the choreography. He would film it, bring in professional equipment, and do a whole deal. I wound up directing it myself, designed the music, everything. But when I saw the final print he had put "a film by" whatever his name was— I can't remember.

Brooks: So you actually directed it yourself.

Menkes: I had essentially directed it. The only thing he had done was to edit it and finish it. I had nothing to do with the editing because I had left London to go to California. Anyway, it was very successful. They sent me a print despite the credit issue. I was excited by the film.

Brooks: What happened?

Menkes: I went back to Berkeley to finish my B.A. degree.

Brooks: The press release for *Queen of Diamonds* describes the protagonist Firdaus as a character "whose every hand seems to play out oppression." Did you intend that?

Menkes: Yes. I saw Firdaus as a very oppressed character; I saw her as a drifter, a "white trash" kind of figure. My sister Tinka, who plays Firdaus, made her a lot more than that. But I think she is chiefly a victim. The whole middle sequence with her dealing is similar to the fucking scenes in *Magdalena Viraga*. It's just this endless, endless dealing—seventeen minutes actually.

Brooks: The long shot of her in the casino with the ceiling lights whirling like a merry-go-round?

Menkes: Yes. And that's almost half of a real blackjack dealer's shift. They work forty-five minutes and then they take a break.

Brooks: And she trained for that?

Menkes: Yes, she spent about two weeks practicing.

Brooks: Why the title *Queen of Diamonds*?

Menkes: Diamonds are like glittering jewels that are under the earth; they're like buried treasure. And Tinka's character is like a queen of the underworld. She's a shadow character, very much an underworld character, but she's also like a buried treasure. I think the notion of the female, the value of the "feminine," if you will, in this country is so devalued, so held in contempt that it's like buried treasure. Buried in the sense that no one has access to it. We as women don't have access to it; men don't have access to it because they objectify and degrade women. It's ironic, but the Queen of Diamonds is an unrecognized queen very much like *Magdalena Viraga*. Ida says at the end, "Woe to the inhabitants of the Earth for my people are foolish; they have not known me." I think that that's the feeling in *Queen of Diamonds*: the sense of being unrecognized. The oppressed are never recognized. The important work that they do, that women do, that Mexicans do, and so on, is never valued, never recognized openly. A lot is exploited, but it's not recognized. And I think that on both sides of the equation there is a kind of death.

Brooks: Both sides of the question being both men and women.

Menkes: Yes, or the exploiter and the exploited. I mean, it doesn't really have to be men and women.

Brooks: You mentioned during the Sundance panel on women directors that film should be a medium whereby our culturally or racially determined perceptions are shifted and wrenched. How would you say that *Queen of Diamonds* does this?

Menkes: Well, for one thing, I think *Queen of Diamonds* is my most advanced film in that, unlike *Magdalena Viraga*, it doesn't have a moral point of view. It doesn't let you orient morally. It doesn't let you orient in terms of story and it doesn't let you slip into your normal categories. It disrupts those categories and fragments meaning in a lot of different ways.

Brooks: How?

Menkes: Well, I'm not sure in the sense that I didn't make the film consciously with an intent to do that. I work intuitively. But for instance, at the beginning you see this hand.

Brooks: The single hand with the long nails coming out of the bedsheets.

Menkes: And the hand is not contextualized. Then you see this dealer and then an old man. By not contextualizing these elements the film works on you. But people don't want to allow it to work on them. That's why they leave or get upset. They showed *Queen of Diamonds* in the AFI's "Women Make Movies" festival at the Kennedy Center in Washington, DC. There were about four people who walked out of the screening. A few people also booed at the end of the film. Three guys. I wanted to ask them, "What is bugging you here?" But I didn't get an opportunity. I think that people want to put things in understandable categories. Categories that are familiar. And there are not really familiar categories in *Queen of Diamonds*. It all feels like it doesn't connect, and yet on a deeper level it connects profoundly.

Brooks: How would you say it connects?

Menkes: As the experience of oppression. The experience of being the other has not been explored very much in film except from an explanatory point of view.

Brooks: You mean through the documentary.

Menkes: Documentary and telling about; not *showing*. So you have the film *Absolutely Positive* [shown at the Sundance Film Festival]. They talk about the fact that they're HIV positive, they talk about being gay, they talk about the dysfunctional family. But the film doesn't get into the more profound levels about the experience of being cut off and disconnected. What does it mean to be "other"? What is that really all about? We don't even know. We don't have a clue. I don't think anybody does. But let's say women who are interested in it—I can't look at great works by women filmmakers about this issue because there hasn't been anything done. Even a film like Yvonne Rainer's *Privilege*, which I respect very much, is again *talking* about: it's not *IT*, it's not the beginning of otherness. I think in all my films I've tried to get at it. In *Queen of Diamonds*, I've gotten at it the best in terms of abstracting that experience and presenting it in an unadulterated form. Which is another thing that freaks people out. It's a presentation of an experience without translation, so there's no telling about it. It just is *it*: the fragmentation, the cut-offness, the alienation, the beating the head against the wall. That whole middle section of *Queen of Diamonds*, it's just unadulterated. Untranslated.

Brooks: You said you think that *Queen of Diamonds* gets at it best of all; better than *Magdalena Viraga*. Why?

Menkes: I shouldn't say "better," it's just step three. In *Magdalena Viraga,* Tinka's character, Ida, is a suppressed character who's just beginning to confront her own internalized self-hate and say no to it. Or at least acknowledge it: "Yes, I am a witch." Ida's still dying for some sort of validation from the oppressor. She wants a man to say, "You're O.K. I love you." And she thinks that that will heal her or something. But the point is, she's still very hooked into it. Her main thing is battling against the walls of the patriarchy. And as long as you're battling, you're wrapped up in it.

Brooks: They didn't have problems understanding *Magdalena Viraga*?

Menkes: Oh, they did. But in a way, it's easier to get *Magdalena Viraga*. It's more obvious what it's about. She's oppressed by men, she's angry, she's trying to fight back, and so on. In *Queen of Diamonds* she has withdrawn from the battle. She's no longer interested in the moral question. I think the lack of moral stance is a big issue in *Queen of Diamonds*. People are used to thinking about oppression in moral terms. *Queen of Diamonds* is just this experience. Firdaus has withdrawn from an active battling and she doesn't allow the environment to define her in the way that Ida does in *Magdalena Viraga*. And because of this, the environment starts to decay. There is the sense in *Queen of Diamonds* that the environment is decaying and dissolving around Firdaus.

Brooks: How is Firdaus's refusal to fight related to the environment decaying?

Menkes: The environment can oppress her only to the extent that she gives it the power to oppress her and that she sees it as empowered. The reality is that she's oppressed as a dealer because she has to be in there dealing. She needs the money. But on a more personal level, it's not getting to her. She's not as involved...she doesn't want to prove to the guys that she's beautiful or cool or "Please love me." She's not in that position. She's very cut off and profoundly hurt, but she's not masochistic. That's a big jump into liberation, although some people still find Tinka's character painful in *Queen of Diamonds*. Someone told me they walked out because they couldn't handle the pain of the film.

Brooks: You had said: "I want to restructure how we see things in terms of the feminine perspective." How does Tinka's not fighting back in *Queen of Diamonds* relate to this project? Is it connected to a non-adversarial position?

Menkes: It's not exactly non-adversarial. I think that you have to really let go. And this is so hard, at least for me. Let go of wanting "them" and "it." I really do not want a deal from Paramount Pictures. Really. I really do not want a boyfriend who thinks I'm a little bit gross and kind of degrades me on a certain level. The sort of "every woman loves a fascist" thing. When you really don't want it anymore, you're very far along. When you abandon that desire, and you commit to yourself. But it's a painful road to travel, to let go of it, because you let go, in a way, of the whole world. And then you gain the whole world. But when you're in the process of letting go, it's pretty terrifying. In a way that's what *Queen of Diamonds* is about.

Brooks: I'm reminded of the manipulation of the environment in the film *El Norte*. Does *Queen of Diamonds* critique commercial film rhetoric in the way that *El Norte* does?

Menkes: *Queen of Diamonds* is an anti-movie pretty much on every level. It doesn't allow you to use the normal ways that you're used to engaging in cinema. Even *El Norte* has an obvious point of view you aren't normally shown. It tries to shift your awareness, but it does it through a traditional narrative structure which has a strong moral base. *Queen of Diamonds* tries to disrupt your moral base in the first place, because any kind of hierarchical moral base is going to have the good guys and the bad guys. As long as you have the good guys and the bad guys, you're stuck in that old dichotomy. That's why you get these leftists who are just as fanatically stupid as the right wing. People have said to me that after they saw the movie they felt peaceful and liberated. It was like something "opened in their throat" they said, and they felt peaceful and free. To me, that's the best.

Brooks: The serenity the film evokes?

Menkes: Yes. Because it opens up these categories which are so ultimately reductionist. It's not that I don't believe in the struggle of the undocumented worker. Obviously I do. *Magdalena Viraga* is still very hooked into them. *Queen of Diamonds* is not, although it refers to them. That throws people off, because they want to locate morally even more than they want to see narrative continuity.

Brooks: Do we have a point of view of Nina Menkes as self-conscious filmmaker, constantly reminding the audience of the camera, of its manipulative gaze, warning them not to get lost in the illusion?

Menkes: Well, I would say the film probably does that in the way it cuts, the editing. It never lets you just lethargically get involved. The scenes are always throwing you off. Suddenly it's this scene, then it's that scene. Then it's this scene forever. Then it's that scene, and so on. You're very aware of the cutting.

Brooks: *Queen of Diamonds'* intrusive editing technique creates a kind of narrative wrenching that aborts any possible linearity or plot.

Menkes: Yes. *Queen of Diamonds* does that. Tinka and I work shamanistically, in a way, because our personal relationship gets very much into the films or I should say maybe the films get into our personal relationship. Or both.

Brooks: What do you mean?

Menkes: I mean that when Tinka and I started making films together she became the "creative," the "female," let's say. Like a muse figure. And I as camera and director played the "male." I was controlling; she was evoking. At the same time, we both are women. In many ways I identify more deeply with her and what she's representing, if you follow me. In a typical male-female thing it's just A and B; here it's like A and B, but at the same time I'm also B. I have a lot of the issues of self-hate that she has.

Brooks: "She" as a character.

Menkes: As a character. I'm denigrated and held in contempt by the larger culture as an experimental filmmaker. So in *Queen of Diamonds*, we reached a kind of crisis over this dialectic of me *using* her in a way and yet still loving her. "Using her, identifying with her, hating her" reflects this larger problem much more than a personal gestalt. In *Queen of Diamonds*, much of the emotion is between the camera and the figure, and there's a lot of fear and aggression on the part of the camera. This figure, this kind of "Wounded Feminine" that Tinka plays in *Queen of Diamonds*, this dark muse—like in my first film *The Great Sadness of Zohara*—there's an innocence to it. The camera is the watcher, and she's like a muse character. It's still weirdly dark and twisted. But she functioned as an embodiment of the "Damaged Creative" or the "Wounded Feminine." The difference between, let's say, most male-female/director-actor relationships, these famous ones, like Bergman and Liv Ullman, and Fellini, is that their relationship never gets problematic. It's probably *very* problematic, but it never *appears* problematic because the woman is this kind of wonderful, creative, magical thing; then, there's a film about this character. It's all very straightforward. It's not tortured. The reason it's so tortured between me and Tinka is it doesn't work in the easy way because I'm also in this damaged position.

Brooks: When I first saw you on the women directors' panel at Sundance, I hadn't seen *Queen of Diamonds*. Then I saw the film. And I thought Firdaus was you. You resemble each other quite strongly. In a way, it's as if you're directing and starring in your own films. How much of these films is autobiographical?

Menkes: Well, none in a concrete way. But all in a metaphoric or a psychic way. I've never been a prostitute; I've never been a blackjack dealer. But on an emotional level, *Queen of Diamonds* is very personal. I see the three films as a slow progression out of a deep exile from self, out of an internalized self-hatred, a progression in a very weird path. This is what I was talking about at the Sundance panel. Without any conscious intention, my work is emerging as a progression, and the spiritual search, the search for the identity of the "Other," the "Female," is producing an entirely different equation. We don't know what that equation is yet. But these three films, *The Great Sadness of Zohara*, *Magdalena Viraga*, and *Queen of Diamonds*, are mapping out an equation that is completely different. Entirely without plan, just Tinka and me working in the dark. *The Great Sadness of Zohara* is the prototype of a spiritual search. She leaves home, she goes on a journey and she returns home. But when she returns, instead of being crowned king or whatever, she's re-accommodated to her secondary status. She's back in the marketplace. And she's pissed. It didn't work. She went out and did all this work and it failed. That was "try number one."

Then in *Magdalena Viraga*, this little "round-trip, Joseph Campbell" routine gets thrown out. *Magdalena Viraga* takes place entirely within the underworld. And Tinka says, "Yes, I am a witch. I am a permanent member of the underworld. I'm not going to the underworld and then coming back, taking the treasure." That whole model is so exploited: here's the hero, he goes into the underworld, he takes the treasure and he takes it home. The underworld is left robbed, and he is left enriched. What about those underworld characters? They've just been ripped off. What is their story? So *Magdalena Viraga* is a little bit about their story. Their story is, "I'm stuck in the underworld and the first, the only thing I can say is 'Yes I am a reptile,' 'Yes, I'm a witch,' 'Yes, I'm here in the mud, yes, O.K. At least I recognize that and I get empowered by recognizing that and it has nothing to do with going home because there is no home.'"

Brooks: Or "I *am* home."

Menkes: Yes, "Home is here," or "I have to transform the environment." That's the next step. And I think that's what starts happening in *Queen of Diamonds*. Firdaus says, "O.K., I'm in the underworld. This is home. I have to start transforming my environment." And it happens in the film—magical, weird transformations in her surroundings, although they're like little eruptions. It's not all over. The palm tree burns; you could say that she almost sets it on fire, that she's burning the palm tree. An upside-down crucifix comes down the street. Jewels suddenly appear in the middle of her house, and that giant dice clock.

Brooks: Is she part of or does she cause these eruptions?

Menkes: I think that she inadvertently causes it by her presence, by her consciousness. There isn't any like A-B causality. But her consciousness of moving from *Magdalena Viraga* to there and saying, "I redefine my world"—that is the only power that she really has. It's in her refusal to see herself as others see her and in her different view of the world. And in her gaze, in her transformational gaze, the environment starts erupting. But it's just the beginning. It's just like little, little kind of buds, you might say.

Brooks: Why did you make her a dealer?

Menkes: Vegas has a lot of these women who are drifters, down and out characters. They go into town, live in these apartments, and they just work. Some of them do it for a long time and they have normal family lives. But many, most don't. So on this level the film can be read as a picture of the desolation of a Vegas dealer. Here in the middle of Vegas, which is such a symbol of the glories of capitalism, is the real thing: behind that blackjack table is sheer desolation. And those dealers are what keep the whole system running. So on that level, it's just another picture of an oppressive situation. But, on a more magical level, there is the burning palm tree and the jewels. And dealing the cards is kind of god-like...

Brooks: The hand of fate. What kind of hand is she going to deal me?

Menkes: Firdaus has a quality of being very powerful even though she's oppressed and grounded. I think that connects to this dark female symbol, this denigrated, creative but unrecognized figure who is really powerful but whose power is veiled and dark. It's not clear. It hasn't come up to air. And actually Tinka, who plays these dark unrecognized characters so strongly, really has this power, on a very concrete level. She's a superb, a brilliant actress—so different in each film. Of all the stuff written about our work, very few people talk about her acting. It's as if even on that level she's ignored.

Brooks: Maybe it's easier to see her ability in *Magdalena Viraga*. For instance, when the warden pushes Ida into the cell, she turns around with this incredible look on her face—twisted in pain. Then she cries. That's very powerful. But it's hard to tell her attitude as a character in *Queen of Diamonds*. What is her attitude in *Queen of Diamonds* when she's bathing this old man in the motel?

Menkes: That's a funny scene. I see her as a kind of messenger from the other side. There are a lot of these old men dying in *Queen of Diamonds*.

Brooks: The only significant male in the film is a feeble, dying old man. Any reason?

Menkes: Right. She kind of nurses him into death. She's messengering him out. You know, like "Sayonara to that old order." So she's like an angel of death. But again, you could just see her nursing him as a side job for the money. And when he dies, she doesn't give a shit. That's the whole thing with the film—everything has a double meaning. I see her very much as a messenger of a new order, but at the same time she's hurting and she's cut off and she's alienated. So it's not the usual set-up where the messenger comes and etc.

Brooks: Apart from Tinka's acting, how do you feel that you convey this hurting?

Menkes: Well, cinematically, there are probably two main devices that make the landscape speak about Firdaus's condition. So that it's not just the regular Hollywood model: "there's a woman in the house and she's crying, so that means she's sad," and so on. In *Queen of Diamonds*, as in all of our films, the whole frame expresses the emotion, the condition of the character—the frame, the length of the shot, the way it's cut.

Brooks: Can you give an example?

Menkes: O.K. Well, there are two main techniques: holding the shot (very long takes), and endless repetition. In the dealing scene and the wedding, we have this cut, cut, cut, but nothing's happening. It goes on and on. And then there are these long shots, like the seventeen minute dealing scene. To me these are two important aspects of alienation. In the long shot, you're sort of trapped and suffocated in this claustrophobic thing that doesn't move. It's as if she's imprisoned in the frame. And then, the other manifestation of the same thing is the endless intercutting, as if you're cut off from some nurturing source, say, your self. So the length of the shots and the way the shots are fragmented is an evocation of emotion. In *Magdalena Viraga* there are a lot of close-ups. I wanted to get close-ups on *Queen of Diamonds*. But as I told you, we work really intuitively, and when I would try to move in—I'd say, "Tinka, I haven't gotten a single close-up of you," and I'd move closer. But I wouldn't like the shot. I'd tell her "No, this doesn't seem right. Better back up." I just couldn't get close to her. There was something wrong. I think it has to do with the nature of the character and the nature of our relationship. The camera, me, my consciousness, or whatever you want to call it was afraid of this figure. The main drama in *Queen of Diamonds* is my fear, my inability to get close to this figure. It's a film about that. It's a film about the fact that I cannot reach this character who is in every single fucking shot. So it's a film about a defensive structure in a way. It's a portrait of a defense in the sense that you want to scream for a close-up, or scream for her to say something at the end of the film, like "Please *say* something!" But no, she's just gone. And once she's gone, it's like she never said it, and you never heard it, and you didn't love her in time and it's too late.

Brooks: At the end of the picture, she gets in the car and disappears.

Menkes: Yes, but the end is ominous. When she's picked up by the car you're not sure who it is. She may be hitch-hiking. She might be killed. And here is another example of the doubleness that the film creates at every step. That's not what happens to the western hero. He rides off into the sunset. It's not a situation as in *Queen of Diamonds* where he might be killed on the road. The film creates this double perspective at every step to show that she can't be that "normal" hero. It doesn't work that way when you're in the "other" position.

Brooks: Would you buy Laura Mulvey's idea that the image of woman breaks up cause-effect linearity in the sense that by centering on Firdaus, you've banished logical narrative movement; you've got one unbroken free association?

Menkes: Well, that might be true, but I don't like to reach that conclusion as a result of Mulvey's ideas. In other works I think it's true that that's how men—or it could be a woman—see things from, let's say a "sexist" perspective. Sexist positioning says that you have this narrative going on and then there are these things that get in the way or that are disruptive, but that are essentially irrelevant to the main line.

Brooks: Right, and these things are usually women.

Menkes: Yes. In a sense that relates to Mary Daly's idea about background. *Queen of Diamonds* is definitely a background movie: the whole movie is background; there is no foreground. So, yes, Mulvey's ideas do work in that way.

Brooks: Your long shots have been compared to Antonioni. What do you think of that comparison?

Menkes: I'm complimented, because though Antonioni is a sexist, he's a great filmmaker, a great visual artist. In the film courses I teach at USC, I give one exercise that's always amazing to watch. At the beginning of the class I ask people: "Write down any feelings you have about yourself as a human being and as a woman, or as a man—issues regarding sex and issues around who you are sexually. Do you have any conflicts?" What always happens is that the women always have these incredible conflicts, and the men are always saying: "I don't get the assignment. What do you mean?" It's no problem; they're totally integrated. I think that for women this is such a loaded question. It's such a can of worms just to be a human being and to understand that you're not a sex object: to really get it.

Brooks: I want to bounce Mulvey off you one more time. She says there are three different looks associated with the cinema: the camera's as it records, the characters' at each other, and audience's as it watches. Narrative film denies the first two in order to subordinate them to the third, the conscious aim always being to eliminate the intrusive camera presence. So the first blow against traditional film is to reinstate the audience's sense of the camera. Does *Queen of Diamonds* address that technique?

Menkes: Definitely. Conventional film wants the audience to forget that there's a camera and to just get involved in the narrative. *Queen of Diamonds* subverts that. It makes you excruciatingly aware of yourself while you're watching it because there's not enough action on the screen to make you lose yourself in the film. It's also related to how Tinka plays the lead in *Queen of Diamonds* versus the way that the star system works. When someone plays the lead in a Hollywood film s/he becomes larger than life. The Hollywood film works by making you revere the star. You think less of yourself, as if the star were superior in some way. Your life seems inconsequential compared to theirs and so you read about them in *National Enquirer* in order to augment your own useless life. The sign of Tinka's genius is though she's the lead—she's in every shot— she's never overwhelming. She has a quality of being invisible.

Even in documentaries about the oppressed, the "Other" characters—homosexuals, or HIV-positive people, or transvestites, or whatever—still assume this kind of a glorified position in the film cinematically. So that, in a way, these documentaries don't break down that glorification of the screen person. Even in a documentary about a figure who's not usually glorified, say, a cleaning woman, she still becomes "This Cleaning Woman," this big charwoman on the screen. In *Queen of Diamonds*, there's a lead character who's not a lead character.

Brooks: There's no visual spectacle, there's no emotion to pull you into it.

Menkes: Right. In that sense *Queen of Diamonds* is a shadow movie, a background movie. We set out to make a film about the background that really is a film about the background, rather than make a film about a background character foregrounded. All my films are about shadow, but *Queen of Diamonds* most of all. The whole thing is about a shadow character and it's a shadowy movie.

Linda M. Brooks *is a critic and writer who was at the time of this interview teaching in the Department of Comparative Literature at the University of Georgia, Athens.*

18

Carolee Schneemann

Interviewed by Carl Heyward

Carolee Schneemann has been one of the most important figures in the development of performance and body art. Meat Joy, *a 1964 performance, and the collection of performance texts and writings* More than Meat Joy *are landmarks in the development of women's performance, and these as well as her other performances and texts demonstrate an unflagging dedication to sexual freedom, exploration of the body as a site for art, and, more recently, animal rights. Her film* Fuses (1968) *has been widely shown since 1968, including Cannes (it was banned from a Soviet film festival as pornographic). A photograph documenting her performance* Interior Scroll *(in which Schneemann, standing nude, draws a scroll from her vagina and reads the text written upon it) has become an icon of feminist body art, encapsulating the sexual, political, and aesthetic concerns of the movement. Her work retains its power to provoke reconsideration of social norms, and texts and images from her performance work have become icons of an art that refuses to stay politely in the conceptual space of the gallery. This interview was conducted in 1993. In 1996 an exhibition of her work at the New Museum of Contemporary Art confirmed the continuing importance and vitality of her work.*

Carl Heyward: I first saw you in 1984 or 1985 in Los Angeles at a *High Performance* magazine benefit with Rachel Rosenthal and Paul McCarthy, at the old Astro Artz building on South Broadway. Do you recall that one?

Carolee Schneemann: Yes I do. It was a benefit performance where there was no prep, no set up; Steve Durland and Linda Burnham, the editors, did miracles. I did not want to go on as part of a group, so I did an extract, "Art Is Reactionary," from the larger work *Dirty Pictures*.

Heyward: I remember the humor, with the pseudo-scientific tracts being read, the slide projections, and you reclining languidly nude on stage.

Schneemann: Well, in "Art Is Reactionary," I am both interrogator and the one who must answer. A double slide projection sets up contradictions, kind of a litany that moves back and forth with different reactions to very short texts.

Heyward: What is your intent in that piece and in your work in general?

Schneemann: Most of my performances start with a mixture of pleasure and rage. Because I am really a painter, there must be some compelling material that I am interested in that can only be enacted live, so I am an instrument. *Dirty Pictures* came out of examining the usual realm of cultural taboos—in this case, it also starts out as visions. My performances usually start out as drawings, certain kinds of information and actions. As the drawings accumulate I see that there is a pressure in them towards making a work manifest. In the case of *Dirty Pictures*, there was a whole series of photographs from juxtapositions that have to do with archaic influences. With these images I find precedents for a more integrated sense of physicality and then I pit that against the taboos in my culture, projecting conventional kinds of erotic images which are what I would usually consider obscene soft porn. *Dirty Pictures* develops a central text intercutting dreams and gendered language. It takes a whole set of gender-specific words in German, French, Italian, and Spanish (the languages that I know) and explores why certain nouns are given particular genders; it's done as a series of questions read by two men smoking cigars and wearing night gowns. It's very droll. It's also metaphoric with a kind of poetic strand that's about "things," how things are feminized and masculinized; paradoxical gender attributions, that's the key to it. For instance in French the female genitals have male genders and the male genitals have female genders. The male performers tell each other that "In Italian the plumber is male and the sink is female. Why is that?"

Heyward: Can you explain the physicality of your work, in painting as well as performance? For instance, your exhibition at San Francisco Art Institute, "Scroll Paintings With Exploded TV," seems not just kinetic, with the motorized mops and continuous video monitors, but also has a sense of a Sorcerer's Apprentice sequence.

Schneemann: For me as a painter, it relates to, for example, the incredible young Asian women walking around in skin-tight stuff at the Art Institute who come from cultures where women are forbidden to use their whole bodies. You have to remind yourself that this is a tremendous breakthrough for all of us. For me as a painter, being surrounded by all sorts of totally macho prohibitions, it was sort of like the joke about the mops— "Hey, man, this is the largest brush in town." Starting out as a painter I was getting double messages: "Hey, you're really talented, but put the brush down 'cause it belongs to us"—that I could go so far but would never be taken really seriously.

Heyward: This message was given by....

Schneemann: The faculty, but mostly the other guys, mostly my male contemporaries. When I entered the art world, I thought that all this would be transcended because we had a shared visionary purpose, but then they were even harder on me, the establishment in particular, the gallery dealers. Although at that time there was a very close corps of mixed-gender artists working together on a lot of supportive collaborative work. At that time I was with a musician—he was an inspiring companion and we were really equals in our areas; sharing what we were creating was of tremendous import to both of us.

Heyward: This was with Judson Dance Theatre?

Schneemann: This was even before that. Before Judson I was working with James Tenney, conductor and composer; we started to work with the group that became Judson. The musicians that he was closest to were Phil Corner, Phil Glass, Steve Reich—all these kids really developed well. Gradually I discovered that my body was a battleground. The energy of that body was always in contention with its culture. In the '60s I was expected to produce children for Tenney, not work into the night building constructions.

When I was young, sexy, it was very confusing to people active in the artworld. It might still be confusing, but then, they could not grant me authority. I was doing big paintings, constructions—in *Eye Body* (1963), I painted and transformed my body as an extension of the painting/constructions. I produced a photographic series with the body painted, covered with string that was greased, oiled, and dusted, all the materiality that was going into these large constructions was then applied to the body which went back into its own forms. It was like an extension, and the question that I asked was: "Could I be both an image in it [the piece] and the image maker?" Could I have authority there? The answer at that time was: "Absolutely not!" It has to do with some conflict still present: why no work of mine is in any museum in America and I have a huge body of work. After eighteen years not finding a dealer or a gallery, I had finally found Max Hutchinson, who had a major, a blue-chip kind of New York gallery. He said, "I love this work, I want to do everything that I can. I see a lot of shows that I want to do with it, but you have to agree to one thing." "What's that, Max?" "You have to agree to not perform in New York City for four years." "Why?" "Because this culture is stupid—they can't accept that you can do both things." If I was Joseph Beuys would I be a national treasure? As opposed to creeping around trying to find another visiting artist job when all my friends are retiring?

Heyward: Not unlike being a black artist. We have our moments, people of color have a moment, women have a moment but it's like we want the whole thing, we want to do our work without having to justify....

Schneemann: Which has to do with the constant evisceration and marginalization of your historic culture or its being usurped into sanitized forms. The other "other."

Heyward: You are a seminal performance artist with a back-log of thirty years of work, at a time when many women are dealing with issues of sexuality and male dominance with greater acclaim than you have been accorded.

Schneemann: What is even more difficult is that young feminist artists and art historians are using my early work—which they never saw—to club me over the head and define it as essentialist and naive, as being less significant in comparison to a whole list of other women whose work they now want to put forward. They use my history as sort of a battering ram or they ignore it. David James just wrote an extraordinary history of contemporary film, *Allegories in Cinema*, in which he did a wonderful piece on *Fuses*, a contemporary re-contextualization of what it's about. I was pleased and proud of that. He asked me when he interviewed me if I had been approached by any of the major feminist film historians, and I had never spoken to or been approached by any of them—not one, they won't touch me. The erotic is analyzed as a construction of patriarchy and is so problematic that there's really no erotic body left. When these historians are confronted with it, especially a "sex positive" body—it's not enough of a problematic, not enough conflict. They are only dealing with female sexuality as a construction...with the contemporary codes of depiction that have to do with deconstructing female sexuality as being inhabited and constructed by male needs, male desire...that's sort of the terminology. I think that it should be deconstructed, and I have been deconstructing it, but from the position of self-definition and erotic power.

Heyward: Power may be the operative word. You use terms like "sacred sexuality" and "sacred eroticism," but power is what keeps coming back to me, your control over yourself, your body, your art.

Schneemann: My pleasure. I have a body that's not conflicted about its pleasure.

Heyward: What would you say has changed in the past thirty years, in your response to a male-dominated society? What has your growth been like?

Schneemann: Wonderful things have happened. When I began, I was obsessed with what I called "missing precedents." When I was eighteen years old, I started to look for other women artists in the world—they seem to have been obliterated. The first research that I did took me into the stacks at the University of Illinois. I would take out these heavy historic books on seventeenth-century nature painting. Each would have in its German or Dutch text an occasional name with a feminine ending...Rosabella or Antonia...I would note the names and it looked as if there really had been some women who had held brushes. That is ancient history now. Once I had a part-time job at The Cloisters. One of my jobs was to polish the plaques under the paintings from the Met. One day a plaque came that said "DAVID" in big letters and underneath in smaller letters: "attributed to Marie Joseph Charpentier," an exquisite self-portrait. When I asked the curator what the double attribution meant, I was told it's a "major David," but it's worthless if it's by Charpentier. It was the first major painting that was seen at the top of the stairs to the Metropolitan Museum. Then I found two obscure Victorian volumes, bound beautifully, titled *Beautiful Women in Art*. This was a survey of painters who had been beautiful women. The only reason that they got to be in a book was that they were beautiful; this lost history was presented as a kind of titillation and that was an important sour discovery.

While still in school I began to do research into visual archaic forms and do a graduate painting thesis based on McKinsey's *Archetypes of the Serpent*, one of those lodestones that yielded great treasures. Fifteen years after I had done the performance work with the garden snakes, I found images of the Cretan serpent goddess; ten years later I understood what they were really doing with those serpents—what those hallucinatory images with stigmata were about. Having been stoned enough and really studying those images, I decided that art history was something that I would make up with my own eyes, and that is the only thing that I will trust, that which I see. No one can take that away from me because they have already taken everything else away. So I began to build these lost historical traces. A lot of them begin to go to lost black culture. In my slide lecture when I address the sacred erotic, I juxtapose contrary images with conventional ones; when I tell the audience "one of these is obscene and one of these is sacred," they get very confused. A great Nigerian Vulva Goddess with staring eyes and clitoral nose next to a Victorian Madonna...it stops the whole thing for them, but for me, there is no question.

Heyward: What denotes that which is obscene and that which is sacred? Societal agreement?

Schneemann: Oh, it's completely coercive, it's suppressive. I had to condense my lecture recently while on a censorship panel to seven minutes. I showed a little votive Vulva Goddess from New Guinea next to a Victorian Madonna figure, marble, pristine. Marble, balanced on one toe, you've seen them—in one hand a baby, tucked against her and in the outstretched arm is a bunch of grapes. She is encumbered with a lot of stuff and her head is up and she looks totally free and exquisite. The little Vulva Goddess is all chunky, scarified all over, with huge staring eyes. This particular Vulva Goddess only goes to her knees—probably she was inserted into the earth—and she has no arms. I told my audience, "In this case I am able to recognize my sexuality, but I lost my arms. On the other hand, I have my arms, but I have no vulva!" My arms are heavily encumbered with the things that males consider appropriate attributes for the feminine, to characterize it. The Vulva Goddess probably did have arms, but they were made of fragile material...

Heyward: Is it possible in the late twentieth century for women to have a clear sense of themselves without having to go through the morass that a male-dominated culture presents to women?

Schneemann: It's what I call "double knowledge" and you have it all the time. You live on what the established culture insists that you function with and then you build in a secret society.

Heyward: You have both a fire and a resignation, your "double knowledge." It's not so much for women to change or for racial/cultural minorities to change, it's for the greater culture to change, those with power to change their hearts and minds. We are viewed at this time as threats, aberrations. Do I have to have a constant migraine headache, walk with a machete, and watch my back all the time? Apparently I do.

Schneemann: Yeah, you do. And you have to watch your front, which may be why we are in San Francisco. It's much like the canary in the coal mine. There is more consciousness and sense of community and people really thinking and chewing through things. It's different here.

Heyward: Artists as wide-ranging as Cindy Sherman, Kathy Acker, Diamanda Galas, Pat Oleszko, and Karen Finley do not come to your defense, barely acknowledge you, and essentially find you an embarrassment.

Schneemann: Not Acker. She would take a positive stand for me, which may have to do with our mediums being so different, she being a writer. But contemporary feminist scholars now use the artists who were influenced by what I did against the meanings of my work. They say that my work's naive, that it's essentialist. They have a whole set of Marxist and semiotic terminologies. It would be of some interest to someday fight them down... they were not there and are mostly younger so they do not fully absorb the erotic and racial transgressions that were in my work then or understand the ironies of the clichés I used that were really strong in the '60s, imageries, things about the Viet Nam war. They are unable to deal with all the pieces that were built around Viet Nam. So they trivialize and reduce the meaning of the body.

Heyward: I have a feeling that they feel your work is topical and trite.

Schneemann: You know, there is an incredible prejudice about the '60s, that "oh yeah you could be impulsive, you could just get it on, you could do whatever you want." So there is an ignorance about the social structures that conditioned the work and that the work reflected.

Heyward: Are feminists prudes or self-protective?

Schneemann: Most of them take the stance that any analysis of pleasure has to first deal with internalization of male desire. Their position seems to be that female sexuality has to be constructed by certain kinds of socially persistent demands and conditions. So I am in the unique position of insisting on the value of my experience as a heterosexual who knows what her pleasure is about, what it consists of. That is not acceptable to the analytic theorists who like to, as I say, stuff their cunts with their brains. They are cut off at the waist, they are moving around fast without all their organs active. Pleasure itself is personally problematic which is what has allowed them to be driven to deconstruct human sexuality. So it is only with Cixous, the French theoretician, that my kind of sensuous insight is put into an analytic position.

Heyward: You have said on several occasions that you trust your body, that you follow your body, that it never leads you astray. Is this close to intuition?

Schneemann: Is it intuition? It's physiology more than anything else. It is really paying attention to how the sexual body is ecstatic and connects to the erotic, which is in itself something that is split and fragmented with two thousand years of Judeo-Christian prohibitions. I trust the body in terms of dreams, in terms of tactility, as a painter—painting comes out of the whole organism, it comes out of having to use the whole arm, letting the whole body be in the "eye," so it does not get stratified or constrained or constricted. This just leads to all these different layers; for instance, hormonal shifts trigger different kinds of dreams, different kinds of energy, different forms of perception that have to do with aesthetic structure for me. Menstrual dreams have a very particular kind of physical impress and power to them—or dreams when you have a fever. The body is going to give you a different kind of imagistic formation when you are hungry, when you are tired. If your lover's leg is on your leg you dream of a log that you are trying to move. So all the ways that the body is informing the energy of the mind is where I start.

Heyward: Would you say that your work is about transformation?

Schneemann: It's about transformation. Layers of metaphor are moving through any of the visual imagery that I am producing. It does not matter what the material or the materiality is, but there is the sense of the metaphor that recharges and is often visually disjunctive. In some sense this work is never symbolic; one thing does not represent something else. The forms impress a whole set of processes and associations that are historic as well as immediate, which have to do with the struggle to imbed the material—the real dance is with the material. Every construction or image I make has to do with the clarification of space as a time figuration.

Heyward: Did your formulations come before the work, or did you recognize impulses and antecedents in retrospect?

Schneemann: Part of this is protohistory, drawing before I could speak. That is an important base for me. Before I was making sentences I was making some forms of drawings. When I was four and five I had some of my Dad's prescription pads on which I did some strange drawings. Any image that I was composing at this time required ten to twenty pages. They were like early flip books. There would be a line, then you'd flip it and there would be two lines and then the lines would be moving into the page left to right and finally the lines would be moving in on the page and finally after twenty pages there would be two crude figures attached to those first gestures. They are really remarkable and I still refer to that process and think about that. So there was that image making that was like something that I *had* to do, that I thought when I was little, that everyone was given something that they made and then you could choose to be something—like I was a "drawer" and I could grow up and be a nurse. Linked to that sense of formation was some sense of my own sexuality being sacred. I was masturbating when I was four and in that experience was where Santa Claus and Jesus lived, in that pleasure in the body. I had that all worked out. So by the time the culture moved in to try to get the pen out of my hand and my hand off my body, it was too late because I knew where the truth was. The rest was not the truth.

Heyward: How do women, girls, who are thwarted from the kinds of investigations that you had the courage and luck to continue, make the adjustment? What was different for you?

Schneemann: Well, my father was a country doctor and there was always a lot of physicality around us: wounded farmers with bleeding limbs, a lot of blood, a lot of bodies that were not intact. There was not the fantasy of the sanitized body in this household. My parents in their relationship were very sensuous, they were very touching, contacting. My father was very wicked and funny, his humor was always very improper but with a great spirit. He would have little jokes where he would bring two green ginger ale bottles to lunch, except one had urine samples in it, and he would just set them down with a little funny smile on his face and say, "O.K., kids, pick your ginger ale!" My mother spent all her life cringing at what the next terrible trick would be. So they weren't prohibitive. There was also growing up in the country; there was a certain amount of spontaneous nudity. By the time I was an adolescent I would be haying, working on the farms. We worked till we were red, red in the face, red in the hands, swollen with heat and swollen with exhaustion. We would go to the river, take off our clothes and jump in. It was not about being sexy—it was just one of those freedoms that were normal for me. When the adolescent kids stripped and would jump into the river, we would definitely be checking each other out, but it did not mean that we would be going crazy and trying to fuck each other. We had a lot of restraints, where we had erotic feeling and where you had just pleasure and being in your body.

Heyward: So what were the limits, the restrictions?

Schneemann: They were constant, just constant, like living in a veil of threats. You did not sit with your skirt up, you did not muddy yourself or run around with the boys. You did not go into their tree house or hide out and disappear for four hours while you played doctor. There were things from outside of the culture like the piano teacher who tried to get up under my skirt, then he disappeared very quickly and I knew that that wasn't right. Or walking on the highway or in the woods and having a truck come to a grinding halt; it's like Thelma and Louise now, but every girl goes through this all the time, some guy slobbering and yelling threatening things and you knew that you had to run away.

Heyward: Do you feel that women are under siege?

Schneemann: Constantly, endlessly. You are always a potential victim and it's going to be your fault because you were walking in the wrong place at the wrong time, you were wearing something that is considered provocative. I was in London after I broke up with my essential companion and I was used to making great love all the time. I would go out and pick up boys— it was the '60s and it was all very magical, but boy, that instinct had to be there or otherwise you might bring home some sadist or somebody who really had a different kind of erotic message to convey. I was always safe because I had this keen instinct.

Heyward: Talk about "Scroll Paintings With Exploded TV."

Schneemann: I have been working with imagery of the destruction of Palestinian culture since 1981. I was doing a series of painted constructions at the time that, in effect, invaded my work. In the series "Domestic Souvenirs," I was using photographs of ordinary things in my life and fragmenting them and moving them into three or four distractive panels so that there were sequences happening simultaneously. At some point I could not afford to concentrate on the ordinary images in my life because of this gratuitous, psychotic invasion and destruction of an unarmed population. It was affecting me in much the same way the Viet Nam war did, with that same sense of outrage. I started collecting newspaper photographs and I started my research, going to all kinds of history books to find out who the Palestinians were, where they come from, where Lebanon had been; I at one point went to the Lebanon tourist office in New York City and they were just closing, I was the last visitor there. They gave me all their slides. I composed a slide lecture of before and after imagery, with inserts from newspaper clippings, which I had to get from English and Italian newspapers, and reports that were coming into the States. I had the slide lecture going and then I began to re-photograph some of the images, blow them up, cut them down. I worked with the destruction of Palestinians and Lebanon for about six years and did a booklet, an inter-cut booklet with before and after sequences. Got into a lot of trouble. Strange things happened. I had a big show of these Lebanon images at Max Hutchinson

Gallery. A company prints and mails all his cards; this was the only time in eleven years that the mailing disappeared. It never got out. They had given me over-prints and I had an instinct, an intuition, and I don't know why, but I started addressing the over-prints. I stayed up till three-thirty in the morning. At that time, I did not know that the regular mailing wasn't going to get out. While we were installing the show, the center panel of a major triptych disappeared; it was stolen, it was just gone, out of there.

Abdul Ahmed and Edward Said came to the exhibit on the last day, and I was very glad that they could see it. Part of the exhibit also included *War Mop* which was a popular work at the time. It was a 19" TV monitor which is attacked by a mop on a very elaborate set of plexiglas cams. It cost a fortune to fabricate this monster. It smashes onto the front of this TV every twelve seconds. On the TV is a video tape, a pan through destroyed villages. The rubble is exquisite—stained glass all washed up and iron works, archaic arches, pink stone—the sea is out on the left side of the image. The camera pans continuously down an empty road and then comes to a Palestinian woman with a scarf around her head who is screaming at the camera. Behind her is her house with her sofa, her bookshelves, her lamp, and then a bird flies through. It's like a stage set. It takes you a little while to realize that the house is only half there, there is no front and there is no side. Everything is surrealistic, almost normal, but it's half destroyed. Collaged with that are before and after slide images, interspersed with very appealing slides of the mountains, people with skis, and men weaving the ancient purple nets from the Phoenician purple—the Phoenicians and the Palestinians are historically linked. I worked with that imagery into the end of the '80s until I was just exhausted. I had the great happiness that Saad Hadad—the fifth columnist who betrayed all his people of southern Lebanon and became an agent of Israel and was personally responsible for an enormous amount of destruction—died on October 12, my birthday, which was a clue that I could not keep going. Also I had no money. I was alone in the house in the country carrying the ashes from the pot-bellied stove to dump them in the snow under the lilac bush. I looked at these ashes and thought, "This is a wonderful material...some coals, some charcoal, and all this dust that still has substance." So I carried the ash bucket into my studio and started doing these empty, empty spills and throws. They were like the essential destruction of the culture that I had just been examining. So that is how the dust paintings started.

These monochromatic dour works began to get thicker. Then I began to incorporate each one into sort of a computer print-out of a lost civilization. I got computer equipment, boards, from a junk shop in Kingston where IBM gets rid of all their ruined stuff. The computer boards were so elaborately soldered, they are like weaving and must have been done by anonymous women or children with small hands...the smaller the hand the more miniscule the paycheck. Then the computer boards began to change and suddenly I couldn't find the bronze-like ones with the dust colored tones. They began to get brilliant and very bright and my dust paintings began to have particles of pigment thrown in. They began to get dense. I became concerned about not repeating my own gestures formally, so I tried to modify my normal gesture with a brush or a roller or the biggest brush around. At some point I began to work with household tools, like scrub brushes, sponges, and toilet bowl cleaners. I would wander around looking for ways to activate the surface even though I was doing all these random motions and still struggling to establish certain kinds of general internal rhythms. I had to have the sense of a coherent internal rhythm that would hold together all this disparate motion and layering. Then it began to get glorious and beautiful and luscious and I realized that they were part of a continuum, starting with the early dark, dour monochromatic pieces, some of which are really just spare, just dust on heavy paper, ashes. They became thicker and larger, pretty soon as large as thirty-two feet. The transition from paper to canvas was very difficult because heavy old paper was so alive; it has a bite, it responds. A canvas holds its surface, it does not give back, does not absorb the way the paper would. That was a formal transition and was kind of tricky. While I am working with the raw pigments, I am thinking about the picture, seeing it.

The unit of TV composition has a strange affinity to acid vision, the same palette, the same primary, saturated high tone that you see in everything when you are on an acid trip. I think about how that relates to the Impressionist palette. Why? No explanation for it really. In the work at the McBean Gallery, I incorporated dust drawings with TV. The drawings are the rectangle of the TV, which explodes and the contents charge the space around it. I had a dream in which I was filming with the video camera and while I was working I saw the images in 5 x 7 prints flopping out the back, escaping the camera, falling off all over. I love that idea that the controlled form is losing its containment. That led to making the video tapes of the dust painting process and inserting certain rectangles in the elongated rectangle on the scrolls—I have a reference—like on the computer boards, I have a rectangle that is blowing itself apart. The video began to introduce the question: "In a video culture what is going to be more actual and immediate...the painting itself and its literal dimension and tactility or the video which compresses the action of the painting in process, but compresses it without any agency?" It was essential that there be no hand, no shadow, and no brush, get rid of the heroic implication, that there would be no self there. It took twenty-two hours to edit it out.

Heyward: In the January 1980 issue of *Fuse* magazine you said you would no longer use nudity in performance because it was no longer emotive, that you wanted to thwart conservative audience expectations, that you are no longer looking for communal ecstasy—that unless the audience can meet your own expectations, there is no communication, no art.

Schneemann: I have constantly been shifting the context in which I will use nudity. My most recent performance, *Ask the Goddess*, is a very funny piece that is didactic but invites a whole set of randomized procedures. I don't want to repeat my old messages; the messages have to change for me to rediscover where the taboos have shifted, because they are shifty in the way that censorship is shifty. So, in *Ask the Goddess*, I am not the Goddess; the Goddess is actually a set of double slides which are continuously projected behind me. The only thing that I have established are the juxtapositions of the slide images, they come out of my own iconography, my own vocabulary of images. They are sacred, obscene, and ordinary objects. The audience is given a set of cards on which they are to write any question that they want to ask the Goddess. Then I have three assistants who carry sets of cards in little strawberry baskets tied to their waists. One assistant has a set of cards which impose physical actions on me; I have to do whatever the card says. Another set of cards has to do with props that have to be involved in this action. Then I have five audio tapes which are given to a third assistant to interject between actions. Whenever those audio tapes are introduced, everything stops. The slides are very volatile, very provocative, and they work like sort of a Tarot deck. The assistant takes a card from the audience; I have to pay attention to the question and look at the slides for the answer. Some amazing things happen, they are just outrageous. Someone asked the question "What should I do about premature ejaculation?" and the slide was a Tintoretto crucified Christ juxtaposed with the most popular Victorian postcard (Isis) image, sort of a mock crucifixion with a woman with her ankles tied together, her hands spread apart and tied on to the cross, and her head slightly drooped. She has soft hair and around her waist and pubic area is a whole section of rope. She invites a kind of necrophiliac approach, she's not dead and all you have to do is take off that rope and you can have her. So I took that question about premature ejaculation in terms of the passivity of the crucified male, and if this is your erotic masculine image, then it is very dangerous to come at all, because you have to formulate sexuality in terms of its sacrificial aspect.

Heyward: You have spoken about the performance artist as shaman. The big problem is the lack of ritual for the coming down of the artist after a performance. The culture does not allow for or appreciate what the performance artist really does or what the psychic or physical toll is.

Schneemann: For all the performance artists who work with radicalizing their own situation—pulling through the real pain of insight about the contradictions in the culture—to really be in your material, you have to go so far away from the ordinariness of your dailiness, there is no provision for getting you back. So that when we come back, we always crash. It's like postpartum blues. After a performance, performance artists don't say to each other, "Are you happy, wasn't it great?" They say, "Are you

O.K.?" "Are you going to live, are you crawling under the bed?" "Can you breathe, do you feel like you are going to survive?" "You are going to make it!" We crash, there's nothing there to bring us back. What the artist needs is to be part of a community that not only appreciates your work but sees that you are in an extremely fragile state and you just might need to be taken to dinner. I mean divas get this, commercial performers are fussed over and taken care of, but the fucking performance artist, you come home and the fucking cat has not been fed, there's no toilet paper, the phone is about to be turned off. It's just a prosaic struggle year after year, day after day, and in this particular instance it's especially sharp and I don't know how to provide for it.

Heyward: You said that Karen Finley has "divine gorgeous rage," but we also lump her in a group of shamans and angry women.

Schneemann: Her divine gorgeous rage is being fueled by very concrete social issues. So that divine gorgeous rage is growing out of really unbearable kinds of neglect and psychosis in the culture. Because it dominates every possibility for us to make a difference or a change to envision something else you have to have an enormous rage. When we were first talking about being Black in a racist society, being female...you can't live that rage out, or you would be a nut case wandering around, babbling to yourself and screaming to people in the streets, "die, fuck you!"

Heyward: There is an equality which is central to your art messages, about the demand and respect for the equality of female sexual pleasure.

Schneemann: Here comes the fire and water; our bodies are the coherence between labor and pleasure, all of a piece. I was raised as a Quaker; there was always an equity, anybody could stand up and speak. The town idiot could stand up and speak with the same attention because everybody was a piece of the human puzzle. Like square dancing, you have your partner, you lose your partner and you get in contact with and are responsible to everybody else in your circle and then you get back to your partner. You are allowed all this intimacy, this physical intimacy.

Heyward: Is there a predisposition for females to be performance artists? Regarding taboos, intuition...

Schneemann: The predisposition also has to do with why the forbidden erotic is always taken by the other dominant sexual culture. The fantasy of the dominant power structure of white male conservative western men eroticizes what they cannot deal with directly in their own experience, what they are afraid of. So they have to displace it. In that displacement you get the fascination and the fetishization of the female as performer, because that's how the male gets aroused and feels that he has power over the image that arouses him—to be aroused, in a way, is to potentially be fucking this pleasure. That pleasure is misappropriately, overdeterminedly identified with the power of white male sexuality. This has to do with why in the art world it would be much more acceptable for a female to be admired and revered and given a lot of help if she was a really amazing dancer, not if she was a painter, not if she was a sculptor. I am talking about in the early '60s when I was just starting out and I thought that it would be all of us together with a vision that had to be explored—but the brush belonged to abstract expressionist male endeavor, the brush was phallic. If you wanted to strip and run around, that is what the males really despised in themselves and had to project outward onto women, and in terms of other performance, onto black culture. The strange combination of sullying and sanitization. Make it filthy because pleasure is always conflicted and then they have to fetishize it by making it more glamorous, more pure, more big, more vital, more expensive. Here comes your poor performance artist who wants to have power over all the available materials.

Carl Heyward is a writer living in San Francisco.

19

Nayland Blake

Interviewed by Anne Barclay Morgan

Nayland Blake is well known for provocative installations, mixed media objects, publications (sometimes in the form of low-cost, photocopied "'zines"), and performances. He has also taught at the San Francisco Art Institute and the California Institute of the Arts / Valencia and has been a visiting artist at many colleges and universities, including the Yale Graduate School of Sculpture and the Harvard Graduate School of Design. His work has been exhibited widely in galleries and museums throughout the United States and Europe, including the 1993 Venice Biennale. Blake's work often explores social / sexual personae, through clothing, puppets, objects, and the implied presence of the artist. His work is often narrative and comic, while maintaining philosophical depth and engagement with the audience. His work constitutes a social intervention through his refusal to deny either his sexuality (in all its erotic, playful, even sometimes infantile aspects) or his intellect, frequently combining both in his very dense, though often very "light" installations. Blake also emphasizes in the following 1995 conversation the importance of artists working together for the creation of a real community of artists, beyond the banal clichés and bland marketing strategies of the "art community." His work in progress, Hare Follies *was presented in 1997 by the Next Wave Festival of the Brooklyn Academy of Music.*

Anne Barclay Morgan: You are an artist, but also an activist and recently a curator. How do you view these different facets of your activity?

Nayland Blake: Well, when I first moved to San Francisco I worked at a cafe and set up an exhibition program there, so that my friends could have shows, so I've been very comfortable with curating for a very long time. In terms of my work, I see myself as a very radical formalist. I feel that if something would be better expressed in the form of a newsletter, then you should go out and make a newsletter and distribute it the way newsletters are distributed, don't make a piece about a newsletter and put it in a gallery. I see my curatorial activity now as being able to engage ideas that interest me but that I may not be able to work out through my own production, that might be better served by bringing together the work of other artists. I see them very much in terms of a continuum. It's the same thing with activism—I believe that if you want to get a new drug approved by the FDA, you go to the FDA and you scream at them until they do something. You don't go make a painting of a tortured person in an interior yelling, and then exhibit that in a gallery and expect to see any real change in your material situation, because there are many social conditions that galleries cannot address.

Morgan: So how do you view the role of your own artwork?

Blake: I try to characterize my own work as the method by which I interact with and come to some understanding of the world. I call it thinking out loud with objects, and it's about my attempt to make sense of my circumstances and to come to some greater self-understanding.

Morgan: Do you feel that that's occurred over time, a deeper self-understanding?

Blake: When everything's going right, yes, you do learn things. Suddenly you can see things in the work, unconscious choices that you made in the work that are pertinent to your current life and to your thinking.

Morgan: What about delight and pleasure in your own work?

Blake: For me, the work can't proceed unless there is pleasure. After ten years of theorizing about popular culture we are stuck with this formulation of desire and how oppressive the notion of desire is. To me desire is oppressive because it's generalized; pleasure is particularized. The point at which people take pleasure is the thing that differentiates the two. I feel like the moments of greatest pleasure in the work can be material moments. It can be the moment in which a particular material finally resolves itself through appropriate use, or it can be the pleasure of suddenly becoming present within the circumstance. That pleasure is closely related to religious pleasure: the sensation of being grounded and being there in the universe. My pleasures tend to be very tied to the intellect. I had a very bookish upbringing; I read a great deal and I'm into the physical reality of books. There's a moment in reading where you're almost in a suspension within the text and then things come together, connections happen. That type of pleasure, that moment of seeing ideas take form is the sort of thing that I want to have happen for the viewer, in the person who encounters my work.

Morgan: I'm curious at your choice of the word "religious."

Blake: I think that we live in a society that encourages all kinds of religiosity, but does not encourage holiness. People somehow imagine that they can have religion without behaving in a holy manner—which is not a holier-than-thou manner. Like everything in contemporary society, instead of thinking about components of our identity as performative, we think of them as objectified. I think that religions, as well as the practice of making art, are essentially technologies/methodologies for how to exist in the world and how to interact with other people. The things that make great art are the things that also make for great holiness. The holiest things are not necessarily the utterances of preachers. There is a confusion. It angers me that certain fanatics in America have made it very difficult for one to have a meaningful relationship with the teachings of Christ. Why shouldn't I have access to those things simply because some people imagine that they have a warrant to oppress and destroy the lives of people around them? Why should I be excluded from those things because I, at certain points in my life, have wanted to have sex with someone of the same gender? The idea that religion is God with a big clipboard keeping track of everybody is an affront. I don't see any reason why we can't have intellect and holiness, pleasure and intellect, holiness and pleasure. All of those distinctions are willful limitations of our lives that are not necessarily accompanied by any meaningful exploration of what they mean. I'm very much for people interrogating their experience, interrogating their existence.

Morgan: What projects are you working on now?

Blake: I'm currently working on a commission for the new main branch library in San Francisco. I'm also curating a show for the University Art Museum in Berkeley called "In a Different Light" and an ongoing catalogue of a number of pieces of my own. Also I'm publishing a magazine called *Bunny Butt*.

Morgan: That sounds intriguing.

Blake: I don't know how much you've been involved with the 'zine world, or self-published magazines, but *Bunny Butt* is an occasional magazine that is about exactly what its title says. Not to make it sound too pretentious, it's an extension of a recent body of work of mine that is playing off of the identification of gay men and rabbits. It's sort of like a gay porn magazine that also has a lot of pictures of bunnies and is about aggressive anality, but it's got a lot of jokes in it. I do it on a Macintosh. It's about thirty-two pages an issue. It comes out sporadically. I make only about 100 copies at any one time. It's not exactly coming to a newsstand near you, but it's a way of exploring a different field. I think that there are really great things about 'zine culture that the art world could learn from. Instead of people sitting around whining about how nobody sees what they do, people who make 'zines do what they need to, get the magazine made, and then send it out into the world through the mail. It's not burdened with a lot of the issues of evaluation and guardianship that overwhelm a lot of the art world. It's a very direct form of communication; it can be casual, intimate, and funny at the same time.

Morgan: And you don't think art can be funny and intimate?

Blake: It should be. But I think all of us are raised with the notion that somehow contemporary art is not for us. Even if we are art professionals, we come to it with a sense of gravity and wariness that we don't bring to listening to records, for example. I teach, and one of the things I make my students do is to talk about records. People are much more willing to be incisive critics of contemporary pop music than contemporary art. People are willing to say that a song stinks in a second and back it up, but they are not willing to say that about a work of art. So everyone guards their responses a great deal. There's a sort of spontaneity in these other forms that you don't necessarily have in the gallery format. There is also the question of intimacy. In the museum context, guards are both invisible and on display. My feeling is that within most galleries what's really being displayed is the viewer, because you are the thing that is mobile within the space. So if you walk in and everything else is static, you become the thing that attracts attention. There's nothing I hate more than shows that have tons of words but don't deal with the actual physical circumstances of reading. It's difficult to read standing up for any real length of time. What a different relationship you would have to that language if you had it at home in bed or on the bus or any of those places where we normally encounter text.

Morgan: Are you planning to make art available on the Internet or through e-mail?

Blake: I use the computer a lot in my work, but I feel like the technology isn't quite transparent enough yet. The methodology of making it is still so present in the way we encounter work over computer networks in the same way that video is almost always less attractive than film. It's always inside a box. Everybody wants technology to be like a pad and a pencil. Once it gets to that point, then the question will once again become "can you draw" or "can you write." In a way, technology is so chancy that the fact that you get something to go from place A to place B is such an achievement that we don't necessarily look at the thing that gets sent.

Morgan: What about your project for the San Francisco public library?

Blake: Sure. Four artists were asked early in the design phase of the building to conceive projects that could be integrated with the structure. I'm working with a list of authors who are in the library's collection, and looking at the mechanism by which names end up inscribed on public buildings. We are democratizing the process more by having a series of public meetings to determine the names that will go on this particular wall in the library in the form of illuminated mirrors. It's a long process. What's important here is trying to make people see a connection between this building and its contents, and understand the richness and excitement of what's actually in this collection. Both the library and the curatorial project allow me to learn how to engage with the process of dialogue, discourse, community feedback. This is the second public commission that I've ever done and the first permanent public commission. It's been a five-year-long project, so I've had plenty of time to start to learn about how you open a space up for dialogue or connection with the community. Not all public art needs to do that, but I think the best public art does. It is frustrating to me that art becomes the form in which that dialogue takes place; really, the design of the building should be the place where that dialogue takes place.

I think most people's frustration with public art is a displaced frustration with their actual circumstances. The thing about *Tilted Arc* is that people were forced to work in tiresome government jobs in an unattractive and depressing environment day after day after day. They couldn't make their jobs better and they couldn't get the building torn down, but they could get rid of the sculpture. That's the sad part of America right now. The public discourse is so limited on the things that really matter to us that we are forced into these ridiculous public discussions that don't allow anyone to be generous, that don't allow anyone to give permission; there can only be discussion about removing things from the environment.

We are at this very weird point in American history where when people talk about "rights" they're talking about negative "rights." They are talking about my right not to have to see that;

my right not to have somebody spend my money on that; my right not to have my kids encounter these ideas. Somehow, we have lost the ability to talk about rights in an expansive, generous, performative sense. A big part of our mood nationally is that people are frustrated. All of this information is coming at them from different places, but they can have very little effect on any of it. Their ability to make changes in their lives is incredibly limited, yet they're expected to be concerned about things all over the world.

Morgan: Do you feel that in your own artwork that you can affect the world, or your environment, the community, to the point of your "generosity," "holiness," and "pleasure," three very positive words that you've used to describe your work?

Blake: I think that would be one's hope, to be able to accomplish that. The way to do it is by example. I don't think that it can be legislated. You can't trick people into being good. I think you can only be good and then hope that will have an effect. In terms of artwork I think that one of the ways that generosity operates is that good work calls for other work. When you see a piece and you want to go to your studio and work—the great pieces of art have always done that. It is the thing that keeps us going. At the Russian show at the Guggenheim a while back I was not very moved by the paintings or sculpture; what was really moving to me was the dishware and the books and the textiles. These things seemed to really do what revolutionary art wants to do, which is to make you look at the object and say, "God, I want to live in the environment or the society where this stuff is around me all the time. I want to be in this circumstance." Revolutionary art wants to give you an idea of what your life could be, and I don't necessarily believe that that is best demonstrated in painting or sculpture. Sometimes it's best performed in a song, or in a plate or place setting. So I think my own mission as an artist is to try to understand how things function; how ideas come into being; how they determine form; how people receive those ideas. There's an entire level of the discussion that gets omitted, which is not what popular culture does but what people do with popular culture.

Morgan: Going back to your show, "In a Different Light," I'm intrigued by the premise of mixing different approaches to a topic.

Blake: The show examines the interaction between queer and straight culture, primarily over the past thirty years, but with some objects going as far back as the teens. There are both queer (gay/lesbian) and straight artists in the show. The reason for that is that many times now groups of people who have been disenfranchised are finally achieving a certain level of recognition or inclusion within the discussion of art, but a lot of times that position is very prescribed. You will be heard only for those parts of your work that everyone agrees correspond to the concerns of a gay man today, or a person of color. It's never, "As a person of color, I want to say that the value of Donald Judd is that he does not deal with weight." We can't imagine that a person of color would ever be concerned with such a thing. So this show is attempting to break down those expectations of what queer artists are concerned with. Instead of curators with a thesis filling in the work to meet that thesis, basically proving ourselves right because there was no possibility we could be proved wrong, we decided to think about groups of works that we were interested in seeing together. So this show, although it is the first major museum show that will contain the work of many queer artists, is not the blockbuster gay art show and it is not a representative show of the entirety of the production of the work of gay and lesbian artists. I feel like that's very important to say up front because that show should take place, but my research indicates that at this point the only institution that could conceivably mount such a show would be the National Gallery. There are simply too many self-identified gay/lesbian people out there making work.

Morgan: Will the works deal with certain topical issues such as mortality?

Blake: The works are split into two thematics: "The Bride" and "The Orgy." Within each of these thematics there are subgroupings of eight to ten objects. Each group may be dealing with a sexual issue, or a formal issue, or a methodological issue or an idea about mortality. But it isn't, "Gay men die of AIDS so here's a picture about death because now gay men can talk about death." It used to be that gay men could only talk about ogling other gay men. That was the only thing to be understood as gay content. Then because of AIDS, we understood that, "Oh well, also gay men can be concerned with the fact that they're going to die." What this show says is that you don't know what queer people are concerned with, we don't know. We can only bring together groups of queer people in different combinations and see what sort of affinities their work may have.

Morgan: It sounds like an exploratory exhibition, but at the same time it seems to be about moving toward that kind of unity that we were talking about earlier.

Blake: I think that in general people are very tired of identity politics. The artists are tired of it, both those who are self-identified and those who are not. We need to come to some point beyond the acknowledgment and tolerance of diversity, which has been the aim of most civil rights movements. We need to move to understanding diversity and delighting in it. I think that is something that we as a people are very far from, because we seem to very quickly forget the possibilities for a connection when we have our backs against the wall. We have had our backs against the wall for nearly fourteen years in a very specific way. The Reagan administration set about dismantling the social and emotional social fabric of the United States. As a result they have bred embattled enclaves of suburbanites who live in desperate fear that their containment strategies (e.g., of people of color, or the poor) will fail and that they will be overrun and their children won't have anything to look forward to but chaos. That entire mindset was fostered by this Republican administration for twelve years. That blatant attack on the social fabric of this country has really been devastating and I do not see any leader attempting to address that. I see leaders attempting to argue for their own dignity within their difference, but not in any sense being able to argue for the reweaving of our social fabric.

Morgan: Do you feel that you as an artist can help in this way?

Blake: Well, there's always hope, but again I think it's something that comes from example. How you go about your daily life affects the people around you. What's the point of giving to Greenpeace if you're nasty to your neighbors?

Morgan: What's it like for you to be in San Francisco as opposed to, say, New York?

Blake: I think San Francisco is an interesting city because it's still of a manageable scale. The people do feel like they can have an impact on it. I think that it is, however, a city that has a very difficult time in seeing itself as a producer of culture. Often, San Franciscans like to have culture because that's the civilized thing to do, but they are not as invested in making new culture.

Morgan: Do you see yourself in some better environment for you personally?

Blake: I don't know. I think that as an artist, your main responsibility is to go to the place that allows you to work, whatever that place may be. Certainly I work enough in other places—I have an ongoing work schedule in New York, so I don't necessarily feel like I have to live there to interact with that community. But a big danger that I see in a lot of smaller cities is that the artists completely disempower themselves. They refuse to value the things they have, and they only talk about how they don't have what New York has. What I say to artists in that circumstance is, "You complain about the lack of an art scene. Have you curated a show that has artists that you like in it for a local place? Have you purchased the work of another artist? What have you done for the people around you, to illustrate to them their value?" Things don't happen all by themselves. People have to take responsibility for the art scene that they're in. When I first came to San Francisco, it was a very closed and bitter and embattled scene. And it was only through people coming in from the outside who didn't have the history of these feuds in their minds that the scene was able to open up. But it also takes people behaving responsibly. Have you made opportunities for other people? That is a big part, I think, of how you should conduct yourself. It's not only getting your slides to somebody else, but if somebody's coming through town, do you show them the slides of your friends? Do you tell them about the show that you went to last week that you thought was important or moving? If you're not doing those things, then you're not really participating in the community.

Anne Barclay Morgan *is a video documentarian and art critic.*

20

Postscript—No Loitering: Art as Social Practice*

Maureen Sherlock

Impaled on a rigid contradiction of economic determinism and ideology, art production is either immobilized as a mere ideological representation, or romanticized in a productivist scenario that promises the transformation of society through a revolutionary avant-garde. The first positions art as only a mirror reflection of the means of production, while the second privileges art's modernist heroes as Communards at the barricades. A more sensitive dialectic of history might admit the subtle complex that shapes our common destinies in the temporal nodes of social life, as well as the tenor of our daily world as individuals.

Postmodern critical practice reinvents the horns of this dilemma by creating an aporia of its own: the narcotic haze of a pervasive late capital is pitted against the hedonism of despair in the lost horizon of utopia. It proposes the triumph of the simulacra over a vanquished metaphysical substance, the video bit over truth, pragmatic cynicism over justice, and the commodity form over aesthetics. In the midst of this malaise, some capitulate to cavalier consumption, while others open their hymnals to the revolutionary chant in a restoration farce. As a third alternative, the artists in this collection of interviews from *Art Papers* try to foreground a dialogue between art and its critique as forms of a discursive, perpipatetic practice revealing the

*Information for this essay is taken from *AIDS: Cultural Analysis/Cultural Activism,* October 43, Winter 1987.

fragility of a mere spectacle of freedom and the renewed possibility of the *agora* as a horizontal or dialogic community. Philosophy, like democracy, begins with *agnoia*, a skepticism toward the *doxa* or dogmatism of the totalizing visions of the church and state. Certain discrepancies and fragments throw shadows across the vertical authority of the city. These phantoms are calculated as marginal by the powerful, but as the articulation of an alternative urban narrative by a number of contemporary artists who have begun to dismantle the fictional ideals that ensure the city as a mythic and monolithic site.

We owe to Walter Benjamin's *Arcades Project* our introduction to a theory of the fragment as a method for seeing urban social practice as a materialist history of art and criticism. He seeks in the detail and the debris of history what is really essential in the understanding of a society. His intention is to carry the montage principle over into history. That is, to build up the large structures out of the smallest, precisely fashioned structural elements. Indeed to detect the crystal of the total event in the analysis of the small individual moment (*Das Passagen-Werke*. Frankfurt am Main: Suhrkamp, 1983, p. 575). The way toward the truth is through the rapid-firing images that flicker through the city and which alone make it possible to see the death mask of commodities on display in the frozen dioramas of the museum and the shopping mall. For Benjamin, we grasp the history of the present by a contesting shock from the past, as the past is quickened through its confrontation with the present. It is just such a Brechtian device that both the theory and the practice of an interventionist art hope to initiate.

The artists and writers interviewed in this volume are all committed to wresting a citizenship for art practice in a society where social life is often a fantasia of private consumption and freedom a masquerade of market manipulation. Each of these cultural producers speaks a patois that interrupts the seamless voice of anonymous authority and dislodges the ubiquitous mask of nature with which it legitimates itself. Some of these artists restore an alternate but repressed history of silenced peoples, others prepare parallel texts that dislodge the dominant discourse, still others co-opt public imagery and insert a subliminal semiotic system to work against its grain. All of them are concerned with an urban architecture that, while building an ever-expanding number of pseudo-public spaces, has progressively disenfranchised large segments of the population from their active appropriation.

The streets where social activity takes place may look socially neutral, but in actuality are highly structured and contested terrains. Traditions of use are not handed down complete and inviolate, but rather reflect patterns of careful selection, as well as omission, absence, or neglect. It is better to think of "tradition" as a verb, "to traditionalize," in order to open the possibility of an analysis of the social constraints on who has the power to legitimate. Tradition is always selective, be the process official, vernacular, or fugitive; its systems of transmission operate on "denial and forgetting, as well as suppression and distortion" (Susan G. Davies, *Parades and Power*. Philadelphia: Temple University Press, 1986, p. 17). In 1829, Robert Dale Owen commented on the lack of what we would now call a public sphere: "Neither the churches nor the State house are under the control of the people, the strange unrepublican fact is that while each of your hundred ministers of religion has a public building at his command, the people have not one at theirs" (cited in Davies, p. 32). Things have not improved in the intervening years, we have only substituted different types of manipulated social sites. Constructing merely public spectacles, like corporate atriums and shopping malls, while aligning itself with the chimera of high culture housed in art and opera palaces, commerce commits itself to a class-bound culture while sustaining the illusory democracy of consumption.

The nineteenth century witnessed the middle class' careful separation of an interior home life from public life. Intimacy and felicity are vacated from the streets into a life of domesticity like a hot-house specimen for those who could afford the price of admission. Since the working classes and the unemployed had abominable housing and working conditions, they continued to live out their social lives in the street. Consequently, their lack of privatization was seen to be threatening and degenerate to both the merchants and the moralizers. "People whose occupations depended on the street came under attack. Rag-pickers, food vendors, hawkers, beggars, scavengers, and petty criminals used the street's rich resources but were increasingly harassed by the city watch and laws" (Davies, p. 30). Needless to say, women workers were universally seen as deviants and whores; ladies, after all, stayed at home. Working class men were denounced as foreigners, anarchists, papists and communists.

These same categories of people recur in Benjamin's reflections on late nineteenth and early twentieth-century Paris. He placed the city on the cusp of the twentieth, and pursued its labyrinth constructions over the commodity fetish and the function of idleness in urban life. In "Paris, Capital of the Nineteenth Century," he poses historically complicit or transgressive characters in relation to specific architectural structures of the city: the arcades (Fourier), the panoramas (Daguerre), world exhibitions (Grandville), the *interieur* (Louis Phillipe), the streets of Paris (Baudelaire), and the barricades (Haussmann) (*Reflections*. New York: Harcourt Brace Jovanovitch, 1978). All of these figures are epiphenomena, monads which crystallize the whole allegory of the modern city. More importantly for our purposes, Benjamin also describes certain ignominious people who interface invisibly on its margins including the double placard sandwichman, the prostitute, and the rag-picker or *chiffonier*. Each is dispossessed by the city of power, but each also repossesses it by establishing a different kind of map through the street traffic. These people are the homeless and shifting nomads within capital, a *lumpenproletariat* despised by the burghers, the revolutionaries, and the utopians alike.

The resistance and survival techniques of Benjamin's Parisian nomads are analogous to the type of art practice with which we are concerned here. These artists interrupt and intervene in the city at what Krzysztof Wodiczko calls "the hour of the dogs": those times when people emerge in the dark parks and streets of the city to contest its daylight definitions and reclaim or acclaim another social meaning for themselves. In inserting their corrosive fragments into this continuous web of the city's infrastructure, these artists and rag-pickers engage in an urban guerrilla war of search and subvert. These invisible citizens, excluded or denied by the economy of power and its spectacular emerald city, offer another scenario of accumulation while collecting the city's detritus of aluminum cans and castaway images. Each understands the empowering tenet here enunciated by T.J. Clark in his *The Painting of Modern Life*: "The spectacle is never an image mounted securely and finally in place; it is always an account of the world competing with others, and meeting the resistance of different, sometimes tenacious forms of social practice" (New York: Knopf, 1984, p. 36). These artists have no time for cynicism or despair, but plenty of time for idling about to spot the fissures in the familiar and the familial. For them, the street is neither a mere vector from one place to another, nor an exotic spectacle to be seen. Each pursues a certain politics of loitering (Cf. Susan Buck-Morss, *The Dialectics of Seeing*. Cambridge: MIT Press, 1989) which permits them the time and the focus to observe the city, not as tourists, but as sociologists of the street. Their irony is not predicated on an existential dread, but on a macabre sense of humor which usurps the ideology of permanence as a vanguard of change. Theirs is not the logic of the supplement, but an alternative rush hour route through the forest of signs. Practitioners in the field of everyday life, they focus on the attended rejects of economic and ideological dissemination, the borderland geographies of shifting meaning. "It is precisely when they no longer circulate, as well-behaved commodities should, that things begin to give signs to a more subversive potential...it takes an unsalvageable existence to salvage the unsalvageable" (Irving Wohlfarth, "The Historian as Chiffonier," in *New German Critique*, #39, Fall 1986, pp. 144 , 148). Unvanquished by even extreme poverty and abjection, homeless men and women, for example, who endure the calculated indifference of late capital have much to teach the privileged but often jaded *bricoleurs* of art at the millennium.

To install art as a truly social practice we must turn to those defining urban spaces where Benjamin says we will find the truth of humanity: "where the walls and quays, the places to pause, the collections and the rubbish, the railings and the squares, the arcades and the kiosks, teach a language so singular that our relations to people attain, in that world of things, the depth of a sleep in which the dream image waits to show the people their true faces" (*One-Way Street*. Harcourt Brace Jovanovich, 1979, p. 318). It was these interactive spaces which the Paris Commune of 1871 sought to retrieve from the image city of Baron von Haussmann. While modernism valorized expressionism as the truth of the individual artist's affective life, the modernist avant-garde continually attacked its presuppositions through both the critical distortion of ideological signs and art activism in the street, like Berlin Dada or Russian Productivism. A similar rift between aestheticism (1980s Neo-Expressionist painting and the 1990s recuperation of beauty) and interventionist art (1980s public installations by Dennis Adams or the Homeless Vehicle Projects of Krzysztof Wodiczko, and the 1990s actions in the public sphere by Iñigo Manglano-Ovalle or the collaborations of Riedwig and Dias with street children in Rio de Janeiro).

In this context, we have come to understand expressionist theories of the individual creation of art as the regressive movement of a conservative society which has despaired of the possibility of art as an ideological force for social change. There are, however, possibilities for intervention and collaboration which challenge the existing institutions with neither the naiveté of the romantic nor the commercialism of the cynic. Mass media have for the most part succeeded in making a spectacle of AIDS, operating it as a mask for the punishment of the homosexual body, its sexuality disciplined through abstinence or suffering and death. The state largely proposes money to be spent not on treatment or cure, but in surveillance through mandatory testing of marginal groups of people, including gays, prostitutes, Black and Hispanic drug users, etc. 1987 saw the emergence of a collective called ACT UP (AIDS Coalition to Unleash Power). Pursuing acts of civil disobedience, research, law suits, and community forums, it has also involved a number of collaborative arts efforts. A sub-committee, Testing the Limits, has worked on video productions such as the Gay Men's Health Collective's program *Living With Aids* and a series of *Testing the Limits* videos documenting the problems and the efforts of many different groups in New York City to combat institutional neglect or oppression.

ACT UP has also sought to reveal the cultural construction of AIDS through a collaborative effort of cultural analysis and activism. They have attacked the idealist concepts of art which portray it as something beyond history, eternal and perfect; as in Elizabeth Taylor's truism, "Art lives on forever," which she used to kick off a star-studded Art Against AIDS gala. This conception of art accepts the impotency of artists to effectively intervene in society while raising art's commodity status. On the other hand, ACT UP addresses an audience other than the black-clothed, English-speaking art glitterati of SoHo. They took art out of the galleries, moving through subways, cathedrals, and neighborhoods like apparitions from seventy years ago when the Constructivists called for ART AND THEATER IN THE STREETS.

Artists are well fitted to pursue the critique of the society of the spectacle and to open the doors to an at least temporary and strategic public sphere missing from much of American life. If we open and preserve a dialogic space, we might even be able to listen to the voices not of wealthy collectors and patrons, but of the silenced and the disenfranchised. Then perhaps we might be empowered to collectively create our own possibilities not only in art, but in history.

Maureen P. Sherlock *has written and taught widely on philosophy and critical theory. This article is adapted from two articles published previously in* Art Papers.

Index